I0151083

The Victory of Humanism

The Psychology of Humanist Art, Modernism, and Race
Second Edition

Thomas Martin

Backintyme
Palm Coast, Florida U.S.A.

© 2013 Thomas Martin
ALL RIGHTS RESERVED

Published by Backintyme,
A subsidiary of Boxes and Arrows, Inc.

Backintyme Publishing
30 Medford Drive
Palm Coast FL 32137-2504

phone: 860-468-9631
email: sales@backintyme.com
website: http://backintyme.com/publishing.php

ISBN: 978-0939479-412
Printed in the United States of America
Library of Congress Control Number: 2012956329

To the memory of anthropologist
Claude Levi-Strauss,
who woke me from my dogmatic slumbers.

Contents

Acknowledgments   v

Introduction   1

1   The Body in Mind, Art in Mind   5

2   The Race to the Bottom of the Cave   27

3   Opera: Myth Made Flesh   49

4   Chained at the Bottom of the Cave   91

5   PC: The Greatest Show on Earth   103

6   Modernism's Theology of "Race"   135

7   Conclusion   155

Bibliography   159

Wonders there are many, none more wonderful than Man.

— Sophocles
"Ode to Man," *Antigone*

The king's grandeur and majesty derive from the fact that in his presence his subjects are unequal.... Without gradation, inequality, and difference, order is impossible.

— Le Duc de Saint-Simon

"All men are brothers," said Schiller, but it won't happen in my lifetime... and it probably won't happen for hundreds of years. The men of today aren't brothers to me. They are beggars, slaves, clods. I soar above them as my music soars above the music of my contemporaries. We exist on different planes. For them, that other line of Schiller's would be more to the point: "Against stupidity, even the gods fight in vain."

— Beethoven

At a certain level, humans have the same brain as a sheep.

— Psychology Professor, Harvard University

Acknowledgments

Although this book took only four years to research and write, in important ways it is the result of a lifetime of thought and writing. My first college English professor, Peter Sharkey, made me feel that I had something to contribute, and this was inspiring to me. I kept reading and thinking during the delirium of my twenties in part because of his encouragement.

I wrote to an Oxford philosophy professor that, "The universities are dead." And he responded, "You're right, with a few exceptions." Some of those exceptions are the several wonderful professors who have made courses for the Teaching Company. This company finds the best professors in the West and tapes them lecturing on their subjects. While I had learned only a small amount during the course of obtaining my bachelors degree, I learned an immense amount from the Teaching Company courses, and this book would have been unthinkable without their wisdom.

I would like to thank my parents, without whose assistance this book may not have been possible. I would like to thank my friend Charles Thompson who has been very encouraging of my writing efforts, and who read this book several times in its many forms from infancy to completion. I would like to thank Paul W., who edited my first book, and whose encouragement over fifteen years has been very helpful. And I would like to thank my publisher for being willing to go against the popular current in academia.

During the seventeenth century, while a small group of men were heroically creating the modern world, the universities were still in the dark ages. Today the universities are in a new, taboo driven Dark Age, are "dead," politicized, while a handful of writers and publishers are creating a new, enlightened, and more accurate understanding of human nature.

Introduction

A professor once said that the ancient Greeks saw things with a clarity that we have lost today. When I first heard this, I was not sure if he was right, but after years of research I have concluded that he was correct. For instance, Plato realized that without justice, there can be no peace in a political community. So the next question was, "How to create a power structure that represents justice?" I shall try to show that the Greeks were hierarchical in their thinking, as the West is today, so they realized that, as parents rule their children, the better must rule the inferior to create social justice. Some people are smart and creative, while most are average or worse in intelligence. The founding fathers of the United States knew their Plato well, so they did not create a direct democracy, which had a bad history, but a republic, which at the founding was hierarchical, more so than today. To rise in power and even to vote, you had to be smart. In terms of obtaining political office today, things have not changed that much.

But underneath the political thinking of the founders was a Platonic psychology and culture. Plato believed that the mind or reason should use the will to rule the passions. As we can see in today's technological innovations, mind really is superior or really does rule, at least a good bit of the time, or when we are in our good senses. The passions mostly get us into trouble by creating crime and chaos, while reason allows us to rise above our animal nature and create form: form for our state, form for the arts, and a constructive social hierarchy. As par-

1

ents rule their children, reflecting intrinsic or natural justice and hierarchy, reason should rule the passions to create a natural or just hierarchy in both the soul and the state. The founders were aware of this, and it is one reason that there is a minimum age to be president, and why at the time a citizen had to own property to be able to vote. Owning property meant that one could afford an education, which was viewed as essential for civic participation. It also meant that one was intelligent enough to maintain an estate and a staff of employees or slaves.

People also believed at the time that religion was essential for developing the sense of virtue and a rational demeanor. Virtue and reason were seen as connected. A citizen had to have both. If one lacks virtue, and is prone to anger like a child or wild animal, then one cannot be rational. Virtue was also necessary to stop a republic from degenerating into mob rule. John Adams said that the Constitution was only for a moral population. Benjamin Franklin was aware of this. As he was leaving the constitutional convention a woman asked, "So Dr. Franklin, do we have a monarchy or a republic?" Franklin responded, "A republic, if you can keep it." He was alluding to the potential of a population endowed with natural rights to degenerate into a wild mob. We have seen this come to fruition to a degree since the 1960s.

The natural rights that Jefferson outlined in the declaration of Independence are positive rights: the right to life, liberty, and happiness. By "happiness," he meant the right to live a life of virtue, not of debauchery. During the 1960s, Americans embraced negative rights: the right to rape, murder, steal and take drugs. Excuses given today for such behavior would not have been countenanced during the nineteenth century. Franklin's dire prediction has come true. Much of society has abandoned the moral foundation of the Republic.

William J. Bennett and others have noted a coarsening of the culture. This is putting it mildly. Humans have lived 99.9 percent of our lives on earth as hunter-gatherers, so take a hunter-gatherer, put him in the streets, and you have a crude and swaggering "criminal." Put him on TV, and you have a popular entertainer. Such behavior and the desire to defend it are natural and do not really require explanation. But that some populations have developed virtue, self control, or inhibitions is what requires an explanation.

Who is the culprit here? The decline of the West is too vast and complex to blame any one group. The answer is most likely found in popular psychology and modes of reasoning. As will become clear, the blame lies with natural rights run amok or gone *Rabid* (the title of a movie discussed later). It did not happen overnight, but over a century and a half. By the "roaring 20s," the West was well on the way to its present position.

During the last two centuries, the vote was gradually expanded in the name of greater representation or natural rights. The increasing power of the lower classes produced, by association in the Platonic psychology, an empowering of the passions or appetites. Recall that the culture of the eighteenth century was Platonist and hierarchical. The lower orders and their passions were kept under control by their betters, but by the nineteenth century this started to reverse.

As the lower class became empowered and started to command the government, the passions, by association, started to tell the will and reason what to do. The process happened gradually during the nineteenth century, but was accelerated in the twentieth, with bursts occurring during the '20s and '60s. To call someone today "wild and crazy" is to praise them. In the media and on the streets today, vulgarity and violence are intense, and crime has risen. But this makes the common people happy and the people rule, so critics are muted as we saw with Dr. Bennett's quote.

In short, what we have seen during the past two centuries is an inversion of Platonism. The subject of this book is a description of that process in the areas of psychology, politics, and culture. We see this inversion in all areas of Western culture, from novels, music, film, and dance, to academic psychology and other theories of society.

The cultural transformation during the past two centuries would shock many of the Founders, but not all. Some, like Franklin, predicted some form of self-destruction, the primary subject of this book. There is a bright side. I show, at the beginning and at the end of the book, that the legitimacy of rationalism, and the gratification from Classical humanism are more profound and real than the vulgar and subhuman trash that passes for culture and values today.

I hope to show that a real victory of humanism is possible. Today, it may be found only within the covers of this book, but under the right circumstances it can spread. If humanism was victorious in the past, it can be again in the future.

Chapter 1

The Body in Mind, Art in Mind

I've seen much finer
Women, ripe and real,
Than all this nonsense of
Their stone ideal.

— Byron

She possessed both types of beauty—style and rhythm.
Style is the force of the ideal, rhythm is its movement...
Proportion his song to his nature, and you shall see!

— Victor Hugo
Les Miserables

When I read, it was I who gained knowledge through myself.
Or was it?

— St. Augustine

During the last two centuries, the West has undergone an important transformation in what it expects from body imagery presented in art and the media. This is of fundamental importance for understanding the change during the same period in

5

the West's perceptions of "race." At that earlier time, Western society presented to itself images that celebrated European descent and culture. In contrast, today's visual culture is designed to present and celebrate diversity.

What connects the two visual cultures is an emphasis on the human figure. While today the figure may be out of fashion in high art, overall the figure is with us more than ever because of the rapid development of the media during the last century. Before about 1800, images were expensive and rare, while today they cost pennies and are ubiquitous. Prior to the nineteenth century, there was a clear emphasis on portraying the upper and middle classes while they engaged in gentle and even ascetic activities such as praying, adoring a religious figure or celebrating the humanist virtues of modesty and temperance; angels were the ideal.

During the nineteenth century, with the rise of naturalism, greater importance was placed on portraying the lower class doing menial activities, like farming or even breaking stones. This trend has gone further since the 1960s with increased portrayals of vulgarity in the media. For instance around 1975, the televised situation comedy *All in the Family* was the first in which the viewer could hear a toilet flush. This is mild by today's standards.

Advertisers and film producers today use indulgence, phantasmagoria, and vulgarity to get people's attention, enthusiasm and commitment. Celebration of diversity fits easily into this visual culture since both have a discontinuous nature. The visual culture of the mainstream is no longer self-centered, morally controlled and beautiful, or angel-oriented, but indulgent, vulgar, flamboyant and diverse.

The decline has found its way into scholarship. In a study on Beethoven, an author noted, "since part of the historian's task is to sift through the refuse of the past, what could be a better place to begin this tale than amid the same trash bins in the city that

Beethoven called home for most of his life."[1] When a titanic figure like Beethoven is treated in this fashion, you know there are self-destructive currents at work in the culture.

In order to understand the visual culture of today, we must start at the beginning of Western history to see the extent and psychological nature of the traditional portrayal of the figure. The importance of the figure to ancient and early modern art is due to its centrality in human psychology. This is apparent in that there is agreement or resonance between felt emotion in the body and imagined emotion emanating from dreamed body imagery. The same emotions are attributed to real and imagined bodies, and they refer to each other creating a bond. The emotionally expressive images of the body in the mind or dreams refer to and bind to our own bodies by association with our felt emotion.

Body imagery also binds to our bodies through similarity of physical parameters. Both of these similarities result in people feeling continuity between their own bodies and those that they see. In addition, psychologists have found that babies can recognize their mother's voice, odor, and heartbeat. This results from the first nine months of life in the womb. It creates a special sensitivity and attachment to the human body, and the sense that the body is an extension of themselves. People project when they see a human figure; the viewed figure is experienced as being an extension of the viewer and of having a self-referential quality: this is how we experience our own existence.

As St. Augustine thought, we gain knowledge through our selves. We are prone to explore and express ourselves through portrayals of the figure. Depending on our values and character, we either respond positively or negatively to an expressive or vulgar and diverse emotional vocabulary among people and the visual culture. During Classical antiquity, most people adhered to the ideal of rationality and emotional self-control. This had a

---

[1] Harvey Sachs, *The Ninth: Beethoven and the World in 1824* (New York: Random House, 2010), 6.

profound impact on their portrayals of the figure.

One of the central questions that has vexed art historians and critics since the Classical world is the status of the human figure. From the extreme of the stick figures of Paleolithic cave art to the perfection of Michelangelo, the human form has experienced every possible permutation. But a common fact that is often overlooked by professionals is that it is a persistent and serious theme.

Artists gravitate towards it. While a few artistic schools have rejected it outright, like Islam and modern abstraction, most artistic schools throughout history have embraced the human form because of its intrinsic appeal. Even landscape artists, like Claude, included the human figure. People find emotional self-fulfillment in viewing the human figure and, by extension, in curved forms or ornamentation in the decorative arts. The human body is curved and flexible, and so we resonate with similarly curved objects in the decorative arts or in our visual culture. Whether the figure is in action or in contemplation, people want to see other people. We can find the reason in human psychology.

Fundamentally, the individual unconscious is comprised in part of body images that are taken from the history of one's peer relations or from the perceptions of one's peer environment.

For example, a person will often dream of family members, acquaintances and anonymous people in modern dress. When dreaming, one feels the agreement or resonance between the desires expressed by the bodies in the dream and the desires of one's own body. Thus, when the people in the dream express fear, happiness, or sexual arousal, one will feel this in the body at the time of dreaming and immediately after awakening.

Even while awake and calm, sudden sexual or frightening mental images can instantly evoke those emotions in one's body. Studies have found that humans are hard wired to imitate, and this influences our experience of dreamed body imagery. For instance, neonates can imitate facial expressions. If a person sticks out his tongue, a baby will often do the same thing. And studies have found that children will imitate acts of aggression that they see.[2] If we are inclined to imitate the perceived images in our environment, it is reasonable that we feel and imitate dreamed body images.

Our felt connection with body imagery is so profound that we can mistakenly assume that our own emotions come from society or an external source. This misconception drives much popular and academic thought today about the nature of psychology and character formation. People ask, "Do my emotions come from me or from out there or society?" To imagine that our emotions come from an external source is easy because of the power of dreamed images of the body. As we shall see, the power of dreamed body images can be so powerful that they are experienced as intrusive or confining.

The importance of body imagery and emotion can be seen in gender psychology. The agreement or resonance between male-specific emotions and male-specific body imagery creates a gender identity of masculinity. Similarly, resonance between female-specific emotions and female-specific body imagery creates a gender identity of femininity. Men resonate with male imagery, and women resonate with female imagery. There is a circular relationship between native desire and imagined desire in each case and this leads to imitation. For instance, in the past, women were expected to be dainty, docile, and modest, and men were strong, dominant, or rugged. Heterosexuality and marriage are global norms, so a sexual charge exists in the mind between the dreamed images of the opposite sex and between felt emotion of an individual and the imagined emotion of the opposite sex.

For instance, people can achieve a certain degree of sexual satisfaction by fantasizing about a member of the opposite sex. There is a profound connection and resonance between felt and imagined emotion.

---

[2]Stuart A Vyse, *Believing in Magic: The Psychology of Superstition* (New York: Oxford University, 1997).

Another example is that physical conditions felt while sleeping are automatically represented in dreams. For instance, if you are warm you dream about being warm; if you need to urinate you dream that you need to urinate. I once went to bed with a stomachache, had a dream that I had a stomachache, and when I awoke, still had the stomachache.

The mind can automatically represent the conditions of the body solely with feelings even without perceived images. Imitation is at work here. The mind has the ability to blend emotion with standard images of the body. For example, people can often describe their physical conditions with great accuracy. I recently had a talk with an older man and he went into great detail about his failing health. I definitely felt how he felt about his health. So the mind and language have the ability to communicate with precision subjective states like those that are dreamed and real. Again we see imitation.

Another factor is what we observe. White Americans mostly dream of White people and African Americans' dreams are mostly populated by Blacks. This is consistent with genetic similarity theory. In many grade schools, Asians associate with Asians, Blacks with Blacks, Whites with Whites, and so on, even though there is every opportunity to associate with other groups. Neighborhoods spontaneously self-segregate and are as about as segregated today as in the 1950s.

Resonance and projected desire from a person creates expectations or ideals for himself or herself and for others. And when people collectivise their desires they create norms or social ideals, which are then reflected in the media.

The resonance between felt and imagined emotion is what allows us to detect gender deviance. The body image that enters our senses clashes with the imitative resonance between our own emotions and our own body imagery. For instance, in the film *Little Women* (1949), one girl says to another, "You act boyish." The first girl is making a comparison in her mind between male and female norms. But she feels the emotional clash in her body, which results from an interruption of imitative resonance. The alien behavior/body introduces a dissonant note. Female bodies should exhibit female emotions and behavior. She feels and seeks emotional self-fulfillment in the resonance, in the ideal, and in the harmonious image of another appropriate female. Similarly, when a woman sees an effeminate male, she feels disappointment, or the conflict between her desired image and the image of the man she sees. During the 1950s in San Francisco, city ordinances required women to wear a certain number of female articles of clothing. This resulted from the collectivization of desire.

That memory plays a role is evident in that men and women can imitate each other, but usually rather badly, due lack of resonance. And when individuals feel that their own specific constitutions or emotions do not allow for easy resonance with their official or representative mental images, as with homosexuals, they feel the discrepancy and discomfort. This is an example of the intrusiveness or confining quality of body imagery. Men and women do not really feel social pressure, but rather body image pressure. This explains why homosexuals tend to reproduce heterosexual roles and relationships. It results from a blending of native homosexuality with the power of heterosexual body imagery and emotions. Homosexuals feel an impulse to line themselves up with either one side or the other just as do heterosexuals. We saw this from the girl's comment in *Little Women*. It is an example of the confining quality of body imagery.

After body imagery binds to felt emotion, imagery in the mind, in language, and in public then enforces desires and norms and its patterns or ideals. This explains why homosexuals adapt to a degree to the images of heterosexual norms, and is, again, an example of the confining pressure people feel from images. Cultural norms and linguistic expression result from observing, memorizing, and feeling attracted to patterns in attitude, emotion, and behavior. People do not experience social conditioning, but rather body image conditioning in the mind. As people feel attached to their body image, through imitation, and that of the opposite sex, they feel attached to body images seen in public, and have an impulse to imitate them. This is evident in the popularity of the human image in human-interest magazines. A cross-cultural comparison of developmental psychology makes clear the power of body imagery.

I once was speaking with two 12 year-old Swedish girls, and I was stunned by how poised they were in comparison to Americans of the same age, who tend to be giddy. This reflects that Swedish adults are less emotional and more focused than are American adults. There is a severity to most Scandinavians in comparison to Americans, who in turn are more relaxed. The children's behavior reflected body image vocabulary derived from perceiving adults. Similarly, linguists know that children adopt the accent of their peers, not of their parents. So the general image that is imitated and that comes in from the populace is decisive.

If unimpeded, body image resonance is attracted to the appropriate or idiomatic images seen in nature. As people seek and ideally achieve imitative resonance with their own body image, they seek and achieve resonance with objects in nature. This creates the common impulse to anthropomorphize.

For instance, women are often compared to bunnies and men are big apes. Mammals, such as mice and bears, are more easily anthropomorphized than reptiles and inanimate objects like rocks. This is so even though most people have more experience with rocks than with bears. In design, watches for men are usually larger than those marketed to women. As these nonhuman images, like bears and bunnies, fulfill, to a degree, desire and expectations or ideals for our gender differences, we are similarly attracted to the image of the human figure in general, in areas such as in the media, the public and in visual representation or art. It is, obviously, the most fundamental and appealing "idiomatic" image.

People seek emotional self-fulfillment in the figure in general, both in the image of their own sex and that of the opposite sex. The striving for ideal bodies compels many men and women to try to get a good figure. This pressure can also be experienced as confining. Desire and ideals move from the body into the public sphere, not the reverse. People sometimes think the reverse because of the confining pressure on the self from the body imagery in the mind and public. For instance, if you had a nightmare of being chased by a growling monster, you would experience it as intrusive and confining. Nightmares are more the exception than the rule, so for the most part there is resonance or a positive flow that moves back and forth between self and images in the mind and in public. We will examine later that there are more idealized or, in contrast, more average or realistic figure types in art and in the human population.

If the mind passively mirrored the body then all groups would be similar, at least in the area of gender, and there would be no historical change. Obviously this is not the case, so we must examine the dynamics of change. Because of ideals from other sources than the body, such as from religion and philosophy, people can project different emotions, which are then collectivised and internalized. This results in change or at least pressure on the group and the vocabulary of body images in the mind. Again, there is resonance, and pressure can move in either direction, from images to body, or from body to images.

Before the twentieth century, aggression between peers was stigmatized as uncivilized or barbaric, and gender was conceived largely in terms of social status. Starting during the early twentieth century, aggression became a larger source of gender values in the West, and this changed expectations and patterns of sexual selection. This will be explored in detail later, when we discuss early film history.

Humans are not endlessly changeable in a physical sense, but there is room for change in ideals. We have seen significant change in gender ideals during the past century. Women's natural modesty was seen for centuries to be the feminine ideal, as it was what men found sexually attractive.[3] But this ideal was abandoned during the past century. Now strength is often a feminine ideal, at least in the area of self-reporting. Hence, we have heroic actresses today like Angelina Jolie. These values did not drop from the sky but were adopted from men.

Popular feminism is largely driven by imitation of men, and this is a modern development. Men are not expected to imitate women, but women are expected to imitate men. It is common for women to dress like men, but men almost never dress like women. This relationship of imitation actually grows out of the relationship that existed between the sexes during the nineteenth century. At that time, women were socially male-dependent. They obtained social status from fathers and husbands. They obtained status by an act of imitation. It was easy for feminists to propose that women, in imitation of men, work themselves in the job market to obtain their social status.

Modern studies find that women are still concerned about the status of men, regardless of their own status. Even high status women want high status men and are sensitive to questions of status for men. This shows that women are pre-wired to be status conscious in their selection of men. This makes evolutionary sense, so it will not go away, as we have seen when women obtain official existential independence from men. Even when independent of men, women feel compelled to imitate men in obtaining their social status, because their deeper desire is to obtain their status from being a subset of men, which, as we have seen, is a form of imitation. Even high status women are concerned about the status of a potential mate. They feel that it reflects or rubs off on them, as it did during the nineteenth century. We can see that women's deeper concerns lie below superficial imitation of men in obtaining status in the job market.

This study will show that status is a foundational structure in psychology. Almost every major and minor point will fit into a

---

[3]Nancy Etcoff, *Survival of the Prettiest* (New York: Doubleday, 1999).

hierarchical structure. We will see that hierarchy is as important to humans as it is to any other group-living species from ants to apes.

Feminism derives in part from the application of natural rights to gender roles and relations. If men may have political rights and be economic aggressors, then so should women.

This is a new development, and few thought this way during the eighteenth century, when the concept of natural rights emerged, as people were nativistic in their understanding of gender or sex. Politics and sex were viewed as separate domains, and in fact were viewed as incompatible.

Today, with a new value system in place, Westerners start to feel, project and collectivise different values and this influences ideals and behavior of self and others in part through resonance. Both men and women are more aggressive than they were a century ago as can be seen in the history of film, and with higher crime incidence today than in the 1950s. The mind is not a passive reflector of the body.

The minds of self and others can adopt values other than the natural and positive, and change mental imagery, emotion, behavior, and the ideals that are projected. It could be argued that some cultural ideals, specifically gender ideals, are more natural, desirable, and easier to adapt to than others. As it is easier to anthropomorphize a mammal than a rock, it is easier and more desirable for modesty to be a feminine ideal, at least from the male perspective. Yes, women can be more aggressive, but does this make women more or less attractive? It may appeal to our historically specific ideals for sex roles, or patterns of self-reporting, but does it appeal to our deepest and most universal currents of sexual desire?

For instance, marriages are less stable today, with men and women jockeying for power, than a century ago. Similarly, some ideals are more functional than others from a social cohesion or crime perspective. This will be explored further when we analyze the deep logic of modernism and Platonist psychology as they have developed during the last two centuries.

An interesting example of the desire for physical movement
lies in the historical preference for marble in architecture and
interior design. In comparison to other stones types, the texture
of marble has more movement or apparent flexibility and soft-
ness. This contrasts with the appearance of harder stones like
granite. Some types of marble appear to flow, and this gives it
warmth similar to the living and flexible human body.

One motive for anthropomorphism is a desire for physical
power, a desire to commune with another body and to share its
power. This is common in animal behavior, called "dependent
rank." A lower-ranking individual raises its status by aligning
itself with a higher-ranking individual or, in the case of humans, with the power intrinsic to another body. It is easy to
see why people imagine images like Bacchus, who is stimulating, or Superman flying around the sky and capturing bad guys
and knocking over buildings. Similarly, humans are inclined to
animate non-human objects in order to create a greater sense of
collective power. One of the motives for this is to break our
sense of isolation as individuals, and to create a greater sense
of power against the threat of death. Hence, humans at some
level are attracted to large objects like trees, whales, clouds, sky
and sun, but less to smaller objects in nature. The Vikings worshiped trees as images of endurance. Similarly, we are attracted
to other bodies because of their strength—the stronger the better. Like the Vikings with trees, modernist Americans today
idolize African Americans because of Blacks' imagined greater
strength and size. We shall return to Blacks' perceived primitive
strength later.

Because of our large emotional investment via dependent
rank and resonance, the human figure has been central throughout most of art history. An ancient description of Daidalos, the
mythical founder of Greek art, makes this clear:

> In the sculptor's art he so far excelled all other men
> that in after times the fable was told of him that the
> statues which he made were like living beings; for

they saw and walked, and, in a word, exercised every bodily function, so that his handiwork seemed
to be a living being. And being the first to give them
open eyes, and parted legs, and outstretched arms,
he justly won the admiration of men: for before
his time artists made statues with closed eyes and
hands hanging down and cleaving to their sides.[4]

Another innovation occurred during the Classical period of
Athenian history. Sculptors started to portray the figure in *contrapposto*, in which the figure rests his weight on one leg. This
resulted in an asymmetry with one hip being higher than the
other. This created the impression that the figure was about to
move, thus having greater dynamism. Egyptian sculpted figures
have even or symmetrical hips, creating a more static image.
The figures in our dreams are most frequently moving, and almost never standing at attention for long periods of time.

The ancients were detail orientated, and were concerned
with the development and refinement of the figure. Roman author Pliny the Elder was the first art historian whose works have
come down to us. The focus on the figure is visible in Pliny's observation of the sculptor Pythagoras, "He was the first to make
the sinew and veins duly prominent and to bestow greater pains
on the hair."[5] Regarding the sculptor Lysippos, Pliny observed,
"His chief characteristic is extreme delicacy of execution even
in the smallest details."[6] The ancients often strove to portray
emotions. Regarding the sculptor Praxiteles, Pliny described
how, "There are two statues by him expressing contrary emotions, a mourning matron and a rejoicing courtesan. The latter
is believed to be Phryne. The sculptor's love may be read in the

---

[4]H. Stuart Jones, *Ancient Writers on Greek Sculpture* (Chicago: Argonaut,
1966) 3-4.

[5]Pliny the Elder, K. Jex-Blake, trans, *The Elder PlinyâĂŹs Chapters On
The History Of Art*, Kessinger Publishing. reprint of (New York: The Macmillan Co, 1896), 49.

[6]Ibid., 53.

whole in the statue, and Phryne's satisfaction is depicted on her face."[7]

The human figure was central in the ancient imagination from about 600 BCE to about 500 CE, a duration of more than a thousand years. After Christianization, sculptures were often defaced and destroyed as pagan idols or expressions of the sinful body and the mortal world. They were replaced by flat and lifeless Byzantine icons, and this style dominated art until the Italian Renaissance of about 1300.

At that time, the fleshed-out figure in painting began to re-occur in the work of the Italian painter Giotto. By 1400 the figure in both sculpture and painting became more volumetric. The sculptor Donatello made several of his works with *contrapposto*. The painter Masaccio made the most realistic figure up to that time, improving over Giotto, but his figures were still crude and clumsy by comparison with what was done later in the century. Nevertheless, he did achieve a certain weight that is an important component of realistic art.

By the late fifteenth century, in the painting of Botticelli, there started to be real beauty and grace. Artists by this time had begun to use shading and curvilinear forms. The fifteenth century is commonly called the Middle Renaissance. But, according to Vasari, the contemporary art historian of the sixteenth century, figures still lacked volume, and compositions were overly schematic or harsh. He also said that figures during this whole period lacked freedom, which is another way of describing the overly schematic character of the painting style. Another flaw of this period was that paintings were too busy, or detailed with an overabundance of objects, which detracted from and weakened the human figures.

The breakthrough in art, when it again achieved the perfection of antiquity, occurred at the hands of the triumvirate: Leonardo Da Vinci, Raphael and Michelangelo. With these artists, painting and sculpture achieve a monumentality and

---

[7]Ibid., 57.

idealization that defines the High Renaissance. Leonardo was the first to create a monumental figure and compositional type, around 1480, with Raphael and Michelangelo maturing around 1500. Together they brought true freedom to the figure and composition, and removed the harshness. One way that they achieved this was by omitting excess objects, like the trees and bushes that had cluttered the paintings of Botticelli and others from the earlier century. Now the figure, like Michelangelo's *David*, strode forth in singular glory, grandeur and heroism. Raphael, in his flowing, pyramidal figure groups, achieves *sprezzatura*, or studied casualness.[8] Raphael, with his flowing elegance, is the Mozart of art,[9] while Michelangelo, with his muscular heroism, is the Beethoven of art. Raphael and Mozart, who minimize conflict, are more utopian, while Michelangelo and Beethoven, with their heroism, have more engagement with the world. Notice the furrowed brow of David, as if he is readying himself for the action of battle rather than being portrayed as triumphant.

A critical observation by Vasari is that those artists achieved perfection by only portraying the beautiful. They did this by using the most beautiful examples of the human body or nature. In this way, they achieved idealization or perfection of both body and nature. In fact, Vasari goes so far as to say that Michelangelo was so wedded to the idea of perfection that he had a policy of never doing a portrait of a living person. This would have been descending away from the ideal in the "mind of God" or the human mind, and losing himself in the particular or the empirical.

Michelangelo's faces are described in earlier scholarship as "idealized." Modern scholars use the term "generalized." Both names contain an element of truth. Newborn babies have an in-

---

[8]Pierluigi De Vecchi, "Difficulty/ease and studied casualness in the work of Raphael," *Raphael: Grace and Beauty* (Milano: Skira, 2001).

[9]Patrizia Nitti, Marc Restellini, and Claudio Strinati, Ed. *Raphael: Grace and Beauty* (Milano: Skira, 2001).

nate ability to recognize the human face.[10] They do not respond to other figure types, but they do respond to the human face. Apparently, babies have a general face-type hardwired into their brains. So the term "generalized" is accurate. Yet, because all babies have this pattern, it could also be described as "idealized" due to its universality. In addition, there is a certain nobility in the generalized face, which helps create the sense that it is ideal. Seeing the face that is in the mind takes the viewer above or out of this world and into the mind, the most powerful and noble part of our bodies. Michelangelo also responded to this nobility, suggesting why he never did portraits in either painting or sculpture.

Let us now revisit the body imagery psychology described at the beginning of this chapter. What the High Renaissance triumvirate achieved is a beautiful or ideal figure type, which adheres to our expectations or ideals, and a very wide spectrum of human expression: from the dark mystery of Leonardo, to the beautiful elegance of Raphael and the monumental heroism of Michelangelo. Vasari describes how in the fresco *The Last Judgment*, Michelangelo portrays a wide spectrum of emotion to which people have responded for centuries. Many respond today. The High Renaissance triumvirate set the standard. The supremacy of these artists was unquestioned until the mid-nineteenth-century rise of modernism.

The triumvirate achieved the perfect balance between art, form or mind, and nature. The best of art comes from the mind. The body needs to be controlled or encased in an artistic or slightly geometric media to be raised above itself, to be projected into the mind and thus to be idealized, aestheticized or experienced as art. Real people are too animated and have too many imperfections. Almost all later artists have lost that balance, either emphasizing details or nature in excess, or overly emphasizing art or artifice.

---

[10]Vicki Bruce and Andy Young, *In the Eye of the Beholder* (Oxford: Oxford University, 1998).

One popular idea during the Renaissance was to transform your life into a work of art. This can be seen in the life of the actress Audrey Hepburn. She studied ballet as a child and went on to become the embodiment of grace and beauty during the 1950s and '60s. Her beautiful personality is well described by film critic David Thomas. Here are some excerpts from a longer description:

> [She] moved to Hollywood, where she was a fairy queen for some fifteen years...She seemed English; she had a sense of manners and kindness that came close to grace...She was never happy with men her own age; she made them seem older and crude. There was always an untouched glory in her...Her Oscar [for Roman Holiday (1953)] was generous, but it showed how far Hollywood had been swept off its democratic feet by her outrageous purity...Hepburn was a creature of the fifties: she was sustained by the real-life royalty of Princesses Margaret and Grace (neither of whom matched the actress's perfection.)...Hepburn largely ignored and smoothed away the ironies and awkwardness in Capote's women...The feeling of public loss at her death spoke to how fondly her look and her benevolence were remembered. Retrospectives had standing room only, and Audrey—in eyes, voice, and purity—rang as true as a small silver bell. The great women of the fifties had a character that is in short supply now.[11]

Hepburn's personality was not an accident, but the result of centuries of cultural pressure in the West to be virtuous, guilt-ridden, and self controlled, like a work of art. Of course, since the sixties, as Thomas has noted, there has been regression to

---

[11] David Thomson, *The New Biographical Dictionary of Film* (New York: Knopf, 2010), 439-40.

savagery—with the West's exposure to a violent world, and the extension of negative rights, the excuses that allow some to think that rape, murder and theft are acceptable.

Most thinkers of the seventeenth and eighteenth centuries took a dim view of raw nature. According to Robert Greenberg, an unnamed seventeenth century scientist wrote, "The visible world would be more perfect if the seas and lands made more regular features; if the rains were more regular; if, in a word, the world had fewer monstrosities and less disorder." A French missionary described Niagara Falls as "falling from a horrible precipice, foaming and boiling, after the most hideous manner imaginable and making an outrageous noise, a dismal roaring, really more terrible than thunder." An English explorer described the Alps as, "Hideous, uncouth, monstrous, excrescence of nature." Commenting on these quotes, historian Frederick Art said that, "In the age of the Baroque, they evidently wanted to smooth and regulate all nature and make, as it were, domestic pets of the rivers and mountains."[12] Winckelmann, the eighteenth century theorist of Classicism, succinctly described the import of nature as "vulgar nature."[13] As unformed, it is simply "too much," crude, confining and claustrophobic. Nature's crudeness did not become an artistic ideal until the late nineteenth century.

Westerners once embraced the distinction between nature and culture. Nature *per se* was viewed as vulgar and disgusting, while refined culture was viewed as beautiful and a relief from vulgar, oppressive and confining nature. Eighteenth century artist and theoretician Sir Joshua Reynolds wrote:

> The same local principals which characterize the Dutch school extend even to their landscape

---

[12]Quotes on nature from Robert Greenberg, *How to Listen to and Understand Great Music*, 3rd Edition. DVD lecture series (Chantilly VA: The Teaching Company, 2006).

[13]Johann Joachim Winckelmann, Harry Francis Mallgrave, trans., *History of the Art of Antiquity* (Los Angeles: Getty, 2006), 133.

painters... Their pieces in this way are, I think,
always a representation of an individual spot, and
each in its kind a very faithful but a very *confined*
portrait [emphasis added]. Claude Lorrain, on the
contrary, was convinced, that taking nature as he
found it seldom produced beauty. His pictures are
a composition of the various draughts [drawings]
which he had previously made from various
beautiful scenes and prospects.[14]

Reynolds sensed a certain constricted or claustrophobic feel
to the naturalistic or unformed landscape. The mind gets caught
up in the vulgar details or confining clutter instead of flowing
smoothly over a lucid form, as in the idealized landscapes of
Claude. Outside of the control of the mind, random nature is
cluttered and an imposition. As some experience their own body
image as intrusive and confining, as we saw with homosexuals, we can experience unformed nature in this way. For both
Winckelmann and Reynolds, raw nature is too much or oppressive.

The theme of claustrophobia and oppression will recur in
our discussion of modernism, in both art and politics. To an-
ticipate, this aesthetic of confining oppression will be displaced
from nature to seeing high art formalism itself as confining or
imposing, then further displaced to oppose the confining upper class during the French Revolution. Such perceived confinements will be the primary element thrown off or rebelled
against, to create the new moral and political or hierarchical
and aesthetic priorities of modernism. People started to feel
that form itself and the traditional hierarchies were confining or
oppressive, instead of nature.

To continue, according to Reynolds, the Dutch artists emphasized dark, cluttered, and grimy nature. The Rococo, as in
the work of Boucher, emphasized an overly stylized eroticism.

---

[14]Sir Joshua Reynolds, *Discourses* (New York: Penguin, 1790/1992), 130.

Nevertheless, Vermeer was a master of light, and this has a certain, limited, appeal. In the Baroque, like Rubens or Bernini, the figure was over-animated. There was too much movement, with figures vibrating and tumbling here and there. A Hollywood film from the 1930s shows the importance of a large degree of stillness for art. In the film *Marie-Antoinette* (1938), with Norma Shearer and Tyrone Power, the queen is beautifully dressed and surrounded by her courtiers. A man looks at her and says, "In repose you are a statue of beauty." What is evident in art history is that most artists either expose the viewer to too many details in the object portrayed, as in the Baroque, or they take the viewer too much into the mind as in medieval art. Classicism strikes the balance between the form-creating faculty of the mind and observed detail.

Pornography is not art because it stimulates the lower emotions and appeals not enough to the form-giving faculty of the mind. The mind is overwhelmed by the body and emotion. Perfect art strikes a balance between mind and body or emotion, while porn places too much emphasis on the body and emotions. It is simply vulgar to refined sensibilities before the twentieth century. A Classic Venus is art because it strikes a balance between the lucid form of the body and a slight charge of erotic emotion. We saw this in the comment about Marie-Antoinette.

Vasari said that the Venetians artists could not draw, and this was evident today in their amorphous forms. In order to create a solid figure, the brush strokes must be perfectly blended or invisible, as in the neo-Classical paintings of Ingres. During the seventeenth century there arose an interest in still-life and landscape, but these were viewed well into the nineteenth century as being of lower import than history painting or portraits.

Hundreds of books have been published on art history over the past 150 years. Many describe how artists treat the figure, and the influence that religion, politics and science have had on artists' perspectives. The preceding discussion has been a psychological perspective on why the figure so dominated art history before the twentieth century, and why, in the modern period, the Italian High Renaissance was unique and perfect in its treatment.

Regarding further reading, on Greek sculpture, *The Greek Miracle: Classical Sculpture from the Dawn of Democracy* edited by Diana Buitron-Oliver is an excellent short collection of essays on the subject. On Italian Renaissance art, *Classic Art* by Heinrich Wolfflin is itself a classic. A good general survey of art is *History of Art* by H. W. Janson. Another useful work is *The Nude* by Kenneth Clark (Princeton Univ., 1972).

Chapter 2

The Race to the Bottom of the Cave: The Modernist Revolt In Life and Art

Greece was barbarian, and will become so again from foreign influence and from Nature herself. She is always younger and has a beginning in reference to us.

> — Ancient Greek Philosopher (Ocellus)
> *On the Nature of the Universe*

But every person, surely, is his own god...

> — Ovid

Anointed sovereign of sighs and groans.

> — Shakespeare

Ornament is a Crime.

> — Adolf Loos, Architect

The bio-determinism described in Chapter One was common sense to almost everyone before about 1825. By the early to mid-century, though, perspectives started to change with the rise of relativism and particularism, and the Classical tradition in the arts fell under assault from many of the educated young because they experienced it as confining.

The aesthetic and philosophy of that epoch emphasized nature, and nature as it actually was, not as it was arranged or perfected by the mind, the latter being seen in the Classical landscapes by Claude. Raw, vulgar nature erupted into fashion as people sought freedom from the traditional formal confinements. Landscapes became the greatest expression of human emotion.[1] The Salon of 1824 saw the introduction of the Romantics, and the painting *The Massacre of Chios* by Eugene Delecroix. Commenting on this Salon, art critic Adolphe Thiers wrote:

> The cry for independence [from being confined] has reached the ears of the artists. Each has taken his own path. One loves the handsome form of *Romulus* and of *Leonidas*, or the grandeur and profundity of the painting of the 16th century; another prefers our everyday lives and does not scorn our customs; and each, following his personal inclination, indulges his own taste, offering us different styles and genres... Nothing is more pleasing than the variety that characterizes the present-day school...[2]

...because of its freedom or lack of confinement.

Artists were beginning to find beauty and greatness themselves to be confining, and sought escape into the chaos and irregularities of nature and personal experience. This defines relativism, particularism and the decline of standards.

The statement could have been made by almost any art history professor today. Though it is probably not radical enough

---

[1]Richard Bretell, Museum *Masterpieces: The Metropolitan Museum of Art*, DVD lecture series (Chantilly VA: The Teaching Company, 2007).

[2]Manuel Jover, *Ingres* (Paris: Terrail/Edigroup, 2005).

for some. And Manet's portrait of a reclining, nude woman, *Olympia*, shocked most people who regarded its frank sexuality as hubristic vulgarity.[3] Gustav Courbet was accused of vulgarity for the low emotional tone in his painting *The Stone Breakers* (Janson, 1969).[4]

In literature, it was the time of the realistic and naturalistic novel, such as by Zola and Flaubert. Western culture was descending from the form-giving faculty of the mind to the worst, vulgar expressions of the body, as in the lower-class taverns, dancers and whores of Toulouse-Lautrec. Lautrec had no interest in being confined to mere beauty. He had a more expansive agenda; namely, all of nature, the good and the bad, though mostly the bad and the ugly.

When the French nation accepted a donation of Impressionist art, Jean-Leon Gerome wrote, "For the Government to accept such filth, there would have to be a great moral slackening."[5] The form-giving and elevating aspects of the mind were losing their grip on the naturally base body. But why?

The answer lies in the developments of contemporary political philosophy/psychology. The theory of natural rights promoted a sympathetic view to the empowerment of the individual, the body, and the subjective emotions and raw nature as resonating objects. The traditional confinements, which came from above in the social hierarchy, the educational system, and the mind, started to be questioned and attacked. Instead of artists, like Reynolds, being critical of confinements from raw, unformed and cluttered nature, and looking to the mind for liberation, they started to embrace raw nature as liberating: liberating from the beauty of the human figure and from formalized nature, as had been seen in the Classical landscapes of Claude and the Classical figures of Michelangelo.

The slide to the body and nature was done in the name

---

[3]Ian Chilvers, *The Oxford Dictionary of Art* (New York: Oxford University, 2004).

[4]H.W. Janson, *History of Art* (Englewood Cliffs NJ: Prentice-Hall, 1969).

[5]Chilvers (2004), 356.

of liberating raw emotions from the tyranny of reason, which had dominated the West for centuries. When businessman J. Paul Getty was a child in turn of the century America, he was given a beating if reason and reasoning did not dominate his life.[6] Nineteenth-century German physician Theodore Billroth believed that moodiness "was a form of stupidity."[7] In the 19th-century, it was felt that emotions cloud the mind. And in the 19th-century novel *Les Miserables*, a character tells a man who is melancholy, "I see that you have been nothing but an animal."[8]

Some examples of this traditional perspective on the lowly status of the body can be found in the history of dance. During the nineteenth century, young dancers at the Paris Opera Ballet were referred to as "little rats," and during the 1940s, at the Metropolitan Opera, the ballet section was referred to as "the animal act." Obviously, ballet lovers had a higher opinion of ballet, but compared to opera, it is a more physical art form. Similarly, in the hierarchical organization of the military, during the 1940s, privates were sometimes referred to as "dog faced privates." These priorities are rooted in Platonist psychology.

As Plato described in his dialogue *Republic*, justice is achieved when the mind and reason use the will to dominate the appetites or the lower emotions. Similarly, he argued that social justice is achieved when the educated upper class dominates or controls the ignorant, over-emotional lower class. Plato's hierarchy implied a value judgment, with the upper classes being wise, rational, and under control, and the lower classes being foolish and tending toward emotional indulgence.

This was the concept of class in the West for most of the early modern period. After the Bible, Plato's *Republic* is the

[6] J. Paul Getty, *As I See It: The Autobiography of J. Paul Getty* (Los Angeles: Getty, 2003).

[7] Peter F. Ostwald, "Johanness Brahms, Solitary Altruist," Walter Frisch, Ed., *Brahms and His World* (Princeton: Princeton University, 1990), 32.

[8] Victor Hugo, Charles E. Wilbour, trans., *Les Miserables* (New York: Modern Library, 1862/1992), 629.

most influential book in the history of the West. It, combined with Christian strictures, created a generally ascetic culture. For instance, Thomas Jefferson once wrote to one of his daughters that she should never "regret of having eaten too little." And a Czech proverb says, "Expect nothing, and you won't be disappointed." People of the time believed in rising above or transcending the body by climbing up the divine hierarchy through an active or form-creating mind. Acting like a pig was stigmatized, while acting like an angel and religious observance were encouraged. "Mind over matter" was a popular idea at the time. Manners were valued and taught. People saw moral lessons in the elaborate, beautiful, or formal decorative arts of the time. They thought that confinement of the body by the mind, or of the individual by the group, were good and created social order. This was just after the Great Chain of Being was the dominant philosophy, in which everyone understood their nature and place in the social and natural hierarchy.

While hierarchical and rationalistic perspective dominated popular culture of the middle class and clergy during the nineteenth century, it was eventually eclipsed among the educated, especially the young artists. Historicism, a form of relativism that displaced natural law, began to dominate college curricula by the mid to late nineteenth century, while Freud argued that the unconscious is in control of the mind, and Darwin presented evidence that humans were just fancy apes and that there was nothing divine about us at all.

The nineteenth century immediately followed the French Revolution, with its bottom-up politics of natural rights and equality. The ideal of modernism was that instead of reason and the upper class controlling the appetites and the lower class, respectively, the reverse should be the case. In order to achieve justice and goodness, the appetites, nature and the lower orders should control the mind, the upper class, and the government. Instead of the high confining the low, the low should confine the high. Hence, we see the righteous lower-class whores of Toulouse-Lautrec, and an expansion of suffrage starting during the early nineteenth century based on nothing more than being alive.

Many people were becoming fed up with the traditional confinements. The redemption of the emotions explains why obesity, and hence gluttony, became a growing problem in the modern West. Nineteenth-century composer Richard Wagner said, "the emotions are the beginning and end of the intellect."[9] And Hume famously said that the passions should control reason.

Plato and his theory of justice were inverted or turned on their heads. The lower class came to be viewed as righteous, good, and wise while the upper classes started to be viewed as mindless, hubristic, and evil. This is evident in operas of the time, as we shall see.

The nineteenth century also saw the rise of nationalist movements that focused attention on a bottom-up perspective. Johannes Brahms complained that Tchaikovsky's was elite "parlor music" while his own "came from the soil." This logic generated Marx's economic determinism and his notion of the dictatorship of the proletariat. Marx's ideas have a family resemblance to the Enlightenment idea of popular sovereignty. As eighteenth-century poet Schiller wrote:

> In the work of the Divine Artist, the unique value of each part is respected, and the sustaining gaze with which he honors every spark of energy in even the lowliest creatures manifests his glory not less than the harmony of the immeasurable whole. Life and liberty to the greatest possible extent are the glory of the divine creation; nowhere is it more sublime than where it seems to have departed most widely from its ideal.[10]

---

[9] Ulrick Muller and Peter Wapnewski, *Wagner Handbook* (Cambridge MA: Harvard University, 1992), 594.

[10] Arthur O. Lovejoy, *The Great Chain of Being* (Cambridge MA: Harvard University, 1964), 299-300.

This exemplifies the particularism and the bottom-up perspective that inspired the Romantics and the lower-class revolutionaries. Life and liberty can be interpreted as no more confinements. The nineteenth-century anarchist Bakunin said, "To the destruction of all law and order and the unchaining of evil passion."[11] One cannot get more blunt. This would certainly redeem the lower classes since they commit most violent crimes. In the traditional ending of the ballet *Swan Lake*, good triumphs over evil; in the Nureyev choreography from the 1960s, evil triumphs over good. Regarding the leftist movement Syndicalism, Stoddard noted:

> Syndicalism is instinctively hostile to intelligence.
> It pins its faith to instinct-that "deeper knowledge"
> of the undifferentiated human mass; that proletarian quantity so much more precious than individualistic quality...[and] art is "a mere residuum bequeathed to us by an aristocratic society.[12]

As leftist leader Georges Sorel put it, "Man has genius only in the measure that he does not think"[13] Today's bias against the mind is evident in the findings of a study done on the public opinion of eugenics. As Prof. Glad found:

> When asked if persons suffering from genetic illnesses should have children, the response was neutral, but when asked if persons of high intelligence should have more children than persons of low intelligence, the response was moderate to strong disagreement with such an assertion.[14]

---

[11]Lothrop Stoddard, *The Revolt Against Civilization* (New York: Charles Scribner's Sons, 1923), 159.

[12]Ibid., 174.

[13]Ibid., 175.

[14]John Glad, "Eugenics and the Public," *The Mankind Quarterly, Fall-Winter 2009*, Volume L, no. 1 and 2, 120.

This exemplifies modern resistance to being confined. That
the West was inclined to invert the traditional Platonic hierarchy was sensed by eighteenth century artist and theoretician Sir
Joshua Reynolds; he wrote, in his *Discourses*, that:

> The mind is apt to be distracted by a multiplicity of
> objects; and that scale of perfection which I wish
> always to be preserved, is in the greatest danger of
> being totally disordered, and even inverted.[15]

Similarly, Gill identifies elements of Renaissance thought
that contain seeds for inversion. She noted that Augustine and
Michelangelo:

> saw a potentially ineradicable divide between the
> corporeal and the incorporeal realms, and both de-
> scribe spiritual love in a language that draws its im-
> pact from earthly analogies.[16]

We have certainly seen the impact of the earth during the
past two centuries. The connection in this quote is such that
the traditional hierarchy could be inverted and notions of proper
morals could be used to empower the lower orders or realms.

Translating the terms of today's debate into that of ancient
Greek philosophy, what we have seen during the last two centuries is the gradual triumph of Heraclitus' flux and particularism over Parmenides' *One* and Platonic realism or theory
of forms. Everyone today praises diversity and inclusiveness,
instead of the traditional divisions and hierarchy that directed
life and art to the ideal in the mind. As people once praised
"racial" uniformity, now they praise diversity and anything else
that drives towards particularism and disrupts the norms in the

---

[15] Sir Joshua Reynolds, *Discourses* (New York: Penguin, 1790/1992), 136.

[16] Meredith J. Gill, *Augustine in the Italian Renaissance: Art and Philosophy from Petrarch to Michelangelo* (New York: Cambridge University, 2005),
3.

mind like heterosexuality. Rebellion has become worthy and romanticized, rather than conformity to the best, most constructive and natural ideals from a perfect blending of mind and body.

The attack started early. In the film *The Philadelphia Story* (1940), Katherine Hepburn is engaged to an upright man, and he says to her, "We are going to represent something fine and straight. You are cool and a queen and so much your own. You have a beautiful purity, like a statue." Hepburn protests that she just wants to be loved. The man embraces the nineteenth century norm of human beings striving towards ideal behavior, while Hepburn is more focused on the raw desires of the body and is resistant to being confined to being a mere statue. (She eventually dumps her fianc(e) and marries a drunk who would never confuse her with a statue.)

Today, of course, is there anything worse than being straight or square? These are figures that create form. Nineteenth-century novelist Victor Hugo opposed clear and straight thinking. He wrote:

> A certain amount of reverie is good, like a narcotic in discreet doses. It soothes the fever, sometimes high, of the brain at work and produces in the mind a soft and fresh vapour which corrects the too angular contours of pure thought, fills up the gaps and intervals here and there, binds them together, and blunts the sharp corners of ideas.[17]

As the ideal was to be straight or heterosexual, now the ideal is be a rebel against being straight or confined, to romanticize rebellion and be radical or gay.

The inversion or debasement described by Hugo has made its way today into popular culture and advertising. The screensaver for a Samsung DVD player reads: "Samsung, Digit*all*: Everyone's Invited." There is the ever popular "One World" and

---

[17]Victor Hugo, Charles E. Wilbour, trans., *Les Miserables* (New York: Modern Library, 1992), 744-45.

"One Love." A billboard advertisement for a car reads: "United by Individuality". Another advertisement includes the phrase, "Unlimit yourself." These are examples of rebelling against confinement, and being unlimited like God. They are the norm today. Such advertisements point down to the body instead of up to the form-giving, confining, and hierarchical faculty of the mind.

A shift in political thought during the last three centuries was the transference of governmental sovereignty from the king to the people via natural rights. Following this, divinity, wisdom, and goodness were also transferred from the king to the people. As the king had legitimacy via God and ruled by divine right, now the individual had natural rights that were also divine and had legitimacy via reflecting Jesus. Everyone suffers today or is a victim, as Jesus was a suffering victim. And everyone is good and wise today, just like Jesus.

This is how French revolutionaries portrayed the people in ritual demonstrations.[18] The traditional perspective was that people were evil and could not be trusted. For the traditional king, power derived from God. For people, rights are natural or spring spontaneously and naturally from their bodies, and so this greater stature, in comparison to an endowment, gives them divine status over the king and government. If "nature rules," as we have seen, then so should human nature. As the king resisted confinements of his power, people today resist confinements and want to be unlimited. One political commentator observed that the Left have a problem with the idea of limits.[19] As nineteenth-century writer Frederick Schlegel described:

> It is precisely individuality that is the original and
> eternal thing in men...the cultivation and develop-
> ment of this individuality, as one's highest voca-

---

[18] Jennifer Homans, *Apollo's Angels: A History of Ballet* (New York: Random House, 2010).

[19] Steven Hayward, *The Age of Reagan* (New York: Three Rivers, 2009).

tion, would be a divine egoism.[20]

Woodrow Wilson observed the tendency of natural rights to promote selfishness:

> It is a perilous attempt to train the unlearned and the undisciplined to "live and trade each on his own private stock of reason." Its success is due to the fact that it uses these theories of natural right which chime in with selfish desire and so establishes passion at the same time that it overthrows habit."[21]

For John Stuart Mill, the individual was above the state and to be served by the state.[22] If the individual reflects the unlimited God, then who could come to any other conclusion? Today, hippies who strive toward the natural indeed look and talk like their imagining of Jesus, complete with ideals of love, peace, humility, brotherhood, and poverty. The original idea of Christian brotherhood was secularized into the social and political brotherhood of the Romantics, the early Progressives, and later Leftists. There are different styles of counter-culture today, but being a hippie, the literal imitation of Jesus, is still one of them. A recent book is titled, *The Culture of Complaint*. Jesus had reason to complain, and people try to imitate Him. Westerners today complain about feeling confined. Today, all are the "anointed sovereigns of sighs and groans," as Shakespeare wrote. This is how people respond to being confined or limited.

It is a small step from the imitation of Christ to fantasizing that one is Jesus. For instance, I once saw on television a girl being auditioned for a part in a commercial. During her rehearsal she kept making mistakes reciting the lines. A judge said that

[20]Quoted in Arthur O. Lovejoy, *The Great Chain of Being* (Cambridge MA.: Harvard University, 1964), 307.

[21]Ronald J. Pestritto, *Woodrow Wilson and the Roots of Modern Liberalism* (Lanham MD: Rowman and Littlefield, 2005), 52.

[22]J. Rufus Fears, *Books That Have Made History*, Audio-tape lecture series (Chantilly VA: The Teaching Company, 2005).

while watching her it was clear how nervous she was, and that she was clearly suffering. He had a look of pity on his face as he said this, and the girl kept wiping tears from her face as he described how much she was suffering.

Others in similar position conjure up the same imagery. That there is rampant self-pity today is obvious. It is a powerful force in academic thought. Each academic department studies its own victim on the cross, and often they swap notes because of their similarity. A sports clothing store had a hand painted sign in the window that read, "Your body is a temple, but only if you treat it as 1." Notice that the body here is divine and "number 1." As temples contain God, so now do bodies. It is no wonder that everyone sees themselves as wise, good, and smart today. Another clothing store had a picture in the window of a man and woman facing each other, and below the picture was written, "Republic of Us." For Ralph Waldo Emerson, people were gods, and everyone should be free and equal.[23] No confinements here. Emerson once said, "Build your own world." Today, it is hard to get people to do anything else. This is evident in the subjective bubbles young people build for themselves on the internet.[24]

Today's emphasis on unfettered individuality recalls the traditional intersection of saint and social policy:

> The image of the holy person is a measure of ide-
> als. The saint is a privileged focus of spiritual aspi-
> rations and imaginative creative strategies. As de-
> picted by artists, and by humanists, patrons and re-
> ligious orders, the saint functions as an exemplar.
> In spiritual terms, he or she is the paradigm of oth-
> erworldliness, the privileged connection between

---

[23] Ashton Emerson Nichols, *Thoreau, and the Transcendentalist Movement*, Audio-tape lecture series (Chantilly VA: The Teaching Company, 2006).

[24] Mark Bauerlein, *The Dumbest Generation: How the Digital Age Stupefies Young Americans and Jeopardizes our Future* (New York: Penguin, 2008).

earthly things and the mysteries of the divine. In intellectual terms, the saint is the conduit between the past and the present, the mortal life bringing with it a message of philosophical universals. More concretely, the saint can be the polemically bound embodiment of institutional strategy, the vehicle of the order that claims him or her as founder.[25]

Almost every sentence in our definition of modernism expresses these institutional aspirations for a deified and unlimited individualism. The hippie agenda has been implemented. Victor Hugo, in his mid-nineteenth century novel *Les Miserables*, has a man, who was a participant in the French Revolution, say:

Justice has its anger...and the wrath of justice is an element of progress. Whatever may be said matters not, the French revolution is the greatest step in advance taken by mankind since the advent of Christ; incomplete it may be, but it is sublime. It loosened all the secret bonds of society, it softened all hearts, it calmed, appeased, enlightened; it made the waves of civilization to flow over the earth; it was good. The French revolution is the *consecration of humanity* [emphasis added].[26]

So as Christian anger against sin was a force for progress or purgation of the confining body and nature, now the same anger forwards the progress to popular sovereignty, the new vision of unconfined wisdom or virtue and the lower classes' control of the state. Hugo also describes a homeless child as God. He describes how:

---

[25] Meredith J. Gill, *Augustine in the Italian Renaissance: Art and Philosophy from Petrarch to Michelangelo* (New York: Cambridge University, 2005), 6.

[26] Victor Hugo, Charles E. Wilbour, trans., *Les Miserables* (New York: Modern Library, 1862/1992), 36.

The two children, a little frightened, followed
Gavroche without saying a word, and trusted themselves to that little Providence in rags who had
given them bread and promised them a lodging.[27]

When *providence* is capitalized, it means *God*. Govroche is
later described as being supernatural:

The two children looked with a timid and stupe-
fied respect upon this intrepid and inventive being,
a vagabond like them, isolated like them, wretched
like them, who was something wonderful and all-
powerful, who seemed to them supernatural.[28]

This is a typical description of God.
The worst crime imaginable is to enslave God or beat Jesus,
and this is how Hugo describes galley slaves, who are convicted
criminals:

At this moment the cudgeling, multiplied by a hun-
dred hands, reached its climax; blows with the flat
of the sword joined in; it was a fury of whips and
clubs; the galley-slaves crouched down, a *hideous
obedience* was produced by the punishment, and all
were silent with the look of chained wolves [em-
phasis added]. Cosette [a young woman who is
watching] trembled in every limb; she continued:
"Father, are they still men?" "Sometimes," said the
wretched man [who was a former galley slave him-
self].[29]

As the flagellation of Christ was a "hideous obedience" that
evoked horror, so is this state in the modernist God of individualism. There is no clearer example of being confined. It is

---

[27] Ibid., 828.
[28] Ibid., 832.
[29] Ibid., 788.

difficult to tell people what to do today, even with findings from science that clearly shows the biological basis of "sin," aggression or crime.

Woodrow Wilson literally deified the electorate:

> Wherever any public business is transacted, wherever plans affecting the public are laid, or enterprises touching the public welfare, comfort, or convenience go forward, wherever political programs are formulated, or candidates agreed on,–over that place a voice must speak, with the divine prerogatives of a people's will, the words: "Let there be light."[30]

Babeuf, a nineteenth-century leftist put it clearly:

> You are the people, the true people, the only people worthy to enjoy the good things of this world! The justice of the people is great and *majestic* as the people itself; all that it does is legitimate, all that it orders is sacred [emphasis added].[31]

God is majestic, legitimate, and unconfined. No wonder modernists today think the common people are worthy of empowerment and wise. They claim that everything they do is legitimate. Like Louis XIV, they cannot err. For Henry David Thoreau, the goal of life was self-knowledge gained through assimilation to nature.[32] Modernists could not agree more. A TV advertisement concluded with the phrase "Become a force of nature."

---

[30]Ronald J. Pestritto, *Woodrow Wilson and the Roots of Modern Liberalism* (Lanham MD: Rowman and Littlefield, 2005), 155.

[31]Lothrop Stoddard, *The Revolt Against Civilization* (New York: Charles Scribner's Sons, 1923), 148.

[32]J. Rufus Fears, *Books That Have Made History*, Audio-tape lecture series (Chantilly VA: The Teaching Company, 2005).

During the eighteenth century, people often tracked in their diaries the progress of their souls to God. Today, people monitor the progress of their souls to their so-called real selves, or the bestiality of the body that makes them happy. A school of modern psychology, by Maslow, is based on the idea of "self-actualization,"[33] and an opera production at Bayreuth had the goal of self-realization for the characters.[34]

Enya is a pop musician who has sold 70 million recordings; one of her songs is called Pilgrim (on the CD *A Day Without Rain*) and its lyrics include:

> Pilgrim, how you journey on the road you choose...the road that leads to nowhere, the road that leads to you...will you find the answer in all you say and do? Will you find the answer in you?...Pilgrim, in your journey you may travel far, for pilgrim it's a long way to find out who you are.

An ad for a website had the phrase, "Find your inner everything" and another ad read, "The web, myself and I." As Jesus was singular, majestic, good and unique, and all-powerful, modernists believe that common people are singular, good and unique, and powerful rather than viewed as evil. A major fast food chain has written on their drinking cups, "Made to order because we think you're special." Another fast food chain had written on its cups, "Here's to YOU: A toast to your wisdom, clever drink buyer-you have selected a classic fountain beverage, precisely mixed for maximum refreshment." Everyone is portrayed as Einstein today and deserves power.

While playing Peter Pan on the New York stage in 1950, actress Jean Arthur said, "If I can get over the message that we should all try to be ourselves, to be free individuals, then I'm

---

[33]David Crystal, *The Cambridge Biographical Encyclopedia* (New York: Cambridge University, 1998).

[34]Fredrick Spotts, *Bayreuth: A History of the Wagner Festival* (New Haven: Yale University, 1994).

sure I'll have accomplished what [J.M.] Barrie wanted."[35]   A
television advertisement for a female skin product said, "Everything about you is unique." A recent book is titled *The Culture of Narcissism*, and a recent study on narcissism among the
young has found higher rates in comparison to 30 years ago.[36]

As it was common knowledge that Jesus was all-wise and
innocent, it is a common belief today that people are wise and
innocent or good, and so worthy of sovereignty. The modernist
quotations above imply that common people can do no wrong.
With this kind of cultural power at work, it is easy to see how
the West collapsed into unlimited particularism and inverted the
traditional hierarchy. Now the lower classes are good and wise,
while the upper are evil and mindless. We will see more examples of this when we examine operas and film. What was
low has become high, and vice-versa. Recall from our French
revolutionary that the revolution was sublime. Hence, everyone
praises diversity.

Divine-right monarchy creates one cultural milieu, while a
deified electorate creates another. John Stuart Mill recognized
an intrinsic and rationalistic hierarchy when he wrote, "It is better to be a human being dissatisfied than a pig satisfied; better
to be Socrates dissatisfied than a fool satisfied."[37] It is clear that
the West is turning into self-satisfied egomaniacal pigs.

The transformation, over the past two centuries, of the
West's reaction to suffering is particularly important. The
traditional view was that suffering was sent by God to test
our perseverance and faith, and was an opportunity to achieve
salvation.[38]   Most people had a positive emotional response

[35]David Thomson, *The New Biographical Dictionary of Film* (New York:
Alfred A. Knopf, 2002), 32.

[36]Mark Bauerlein, *The Dumbest Generation: How the Digital Age Stupefies Young Americans and Jeopardizes our Future* (New York: Penguin,
2008).

[37]*Utilitarianism* (1863), ch 2.

[38]Rolf Toman, *Baroque: Architecture, Sculpture, Painting* (H.F. Ullmann,
2007).

to this. During the early nineteenth century Franz Schubert
described how, "pain sharpens the understanding and strength-
ens the mind; whereas joy seldom troubles about the former
and softens the latter or makes it frivolous."[39]   Shakespeare
wrote, "Sweet are the uses of adversity, which like the toad,
ugly and venomous, wears yet a precious jewel in his head."[40]
Such thinking was common in the period, and was part of the
mind-over-matter perspective. Confinement by suffering was a
challenge to be overcome by the mind.

But then by the time of Victor Hugo's *Les Miserables* and
definitely by the Great Depression, suffering started to become
an object of pity, as it was with Jesus.

In the film *Modern Times* (1936) a thief is portrayed as motivated by suffering, like the main character in *Les Miserables*,
and the audience is supposed to pity him instead of reviling him
as a criminal as was normal during the nineteenth century. It is
common today for sociologists to justify crime with narratives
of suffering, such as poverty, child abuse, and ancestral slavery.
This is the thesis of Hugo's novel. Oh! How everyone is miserable today and pities one another! As is evident in the very title
of the novel, almost all 1250 pages of *Les Miserables*, intend to
evoke pity and arouse sympathy:

> Two children of unequal height,...one appearing to
> be seven years old, the other five, timidly turned the
> knob of the door and entered the shop, asking for
> something, charity, perhaps, in a plaintive manner
> which rather resembled a groan than a prayer. They
> both spoke at once and their words were unintelli-
> gible because sobs choked the voice of the younger,
> and the cold make the elder's teeth chatter. The bar-
> ber turned with a furious face, and without leaving
> his razor, crowding back the elder with his left hand

[39] John Reed, *Schubert: The Final Years* (London: Faber and Faber, 1972),
268.
[40] *As You Like It*, Act 2, Scene 1.

and the little one with his knee, pushed them into
the street and shut the door saying: "Coming and
freezing people for nothing!"[41]

It is hard to imagine a scene more miserable or worthy of
pity, reflecting the image of Jesus on the cross. Hugo was ahead
of his time.

Similarly, in an episode of *Friends*, Rachel is dating a man,
and she encourages him to tell her about his childhood. At first
he is reluctant, but she goads him, and eventually he starts gush-
ing about the endless amount of suffering he had endured at the
hands of hostile parents and peers. Eventually he is curled up
on Rachel's lap, and in tears. Of course, this is too much and
she dumps the "cry baby," though she acknowledged that it was
"beautiful" that he bared his soul. As Jesus's suffering on the
cross was depicted in art as having a kind of beauty, a tragic
beauty, now common people's suffering is beautiful, righteous,
and worthy of pity. Every modernists today wants to be the main
character in *Les Miserables*, a Christ-type.

The process of transference of divinity with power can be
seen among the Hellenistic cities of Asia Minor. As Price noted:

> I wish to suggest that the cities established [ruler]
> cults as an attempt to come to terms with a new
> type of power. Unlike the earlier leaders and kings
> the Hellenistic rulers were both kings and Greek,
> and some solution had to be found to the problem
> this posed. There was no legal answer and the cities
> needed to represent this new power to themselves.
> The cults of the gods were the one model that was
> available to them for the representation of a power
> on whom the city was dependent which was exter-
> nal and yet still Greek. By borrowing and adapting

---

[41] Victor Hugo, Charles E. Wilbour, trans., *Les Miserables* (New York:
Modern Library, 1992), 818-19.

this pre-existing model of classification it proved to
be possible to accommodate the new kings.[42]

We see a similar process in ancient Athens during the founding of the democracy. The newly formed democratic organiza-
tions adopted mythical heroic ancestors to create the aura of political legitimacy. Similarly, in the modern world when power
shifted during the eighteenth and nineteenth centuries, divinity and the other attributes of the upper class, like wisdom and
uniqueness, were also transferred and used to make coherent
and justify the new power relationships and justice between the
divine lower class and the oppressive or evil upper class. The
will of newly deified mankind would now empower the lower
orders and the appetites.

The rebels in *Les Miserables* are mostly working class people, students, and vagabonds. Again, the suffrage was system-
atically expanded throughout the last two centuries. Traditional
moral and artistic forms were broken as people rebelled against
the traditional confining definition of social order and beauty.
Instead of using the mind to rebel against, or liberate them from,
the natural confinement of the body and nature, as we saw in
Reynolds, the West started to rebel against the confinements of
the mind. Modernists looked to raw nature and the body as a
way to attack the traditional definition of freedom and beauty.
Instead of imposing order, they started to oppose order. Instead
of freedom through the mind, now it was freedom from the mind
through the body, and through everyone being unique and unlimited, like God, as we saw in the advertisements and other
areas of pop culture. This was the fundamental objective of the
inversion. As it was once mind over matter, now it is matter
over mind. We saw this in thinkers like Marx. Today, the West
has a growing problem of obesity and a self-satisfied population
that is resistant to being told what to do. Most Westerners today

---

[42] S.R.F. Price, *Rituals and Power: The Roman Imperial Cult in Asia Minor*
(Cambridge UK: Cambridge University, 1984), 29-30.

believe in going with the flow, and letting it all hang out. Few today, even among Republicans, are cultural conservatives.

Chapter 3

Opera: Myth Made Flesh

So if the common man is seen as reflecting Jesus, and thus is the rightful ruler, then who is the Satanic enemy? It is the upper class, their morality, aesthetics, and the governments they run. As the devil rebelled against God, and this defined his evil, the upper class during the nineteenth century were viewed as rebelling against the righteous and suffering lower class, and even for inflicting their suffering. Victor Hugo describes the soldiers of the government as "Demons" and portrays the upper class or their representatives as evil. This was a common tactic among French revolutionaries. Hence, today modernists believe that the upper class is evil while the lower are righteous, good, and victims to be pitied.

Suffering is an essential ingredient to this mix. The lower class could never rise in the divine hierarchy or be Christ-types unless they could show that they suffer at the confining hands of the upper class or society: groups, institutions, and norms.

In Mozart's opera, *The Marriage of Figaro*, the lowly servant Figaro is engaged to Susana, but his master, the evil Count, plots to seduce Figaro's fianc(e). Figaro suffers oppression, but he's also a fighter, asserts his rights and ultimately triumphs, inspired as he is by the new, bottom-up, theory of justice. At one point, Figaro says, "Figaro says no." The Platonic will is now used to new ends or moving in a new direction, to crush a new evil up there.

When nineteenth-century composer Gustav Mahler was a child, he said that when he grew up, he wanted to be a martyr. And when opera composer Richard Wagner was a young man, he went into a church, saw a crucifix, and imagined himself being crucified.

In Wagner's ring cycle of operas, the folk hero Siegfried is a Christ-type who suffers to redeem humanity, and battles against the evil power of the aristocracy, or the gods and the moneyed elite. Wagner recycles Christian and pagan imagery and ideas at the service of resurrecting the natural in human nature.[1] Siegfried is Wagner's "ideal man."

Gilroy Gardens, a nature theme park in California, advertises with the phrase, "Where children play on a higher ground." We see an inversion of Plato with nature as high. A contemporary philosopher believes that rocks have the highest or most real existence. This would certainly have appealed to Mozart and Wagner. In Verdi's opera *Il Trovatore*, Leonora says that she will sacrifice herself to save the life of her boyfriend Manrico. Manrico's mother is a lowly Gypsy, who at one point says, "Even the wretched have a God." The Gypsy, Manrico, and Leonora are all oppressed by the evil count, or by upper-class societal dominance and rules. In Verdi's opera *La Traviata*, a courtesan is forced to leave a man whom she loves because the man's father insists that she is too low or morally polluting for his son. She agrees to leave him out of a sense of self-sacrifice. The father eventually realizes that he is oppressing her, or is confining, and encourages the couple to come back together. So we see the triumph of unconfined nature or emotion over society, as we saw in Hepburn's request to be simply loved in *The Philadelphia Story*. No modernist wants to be an example of purity, like a statue or an angel.

---

[1] Joachim Kohler, Steward Spencer, trans., *Richard Wagner: The Last of the Titans* (New Haven: Yale University, 2004).

In Puccini's opera Tosca, the singer Tosca and her painter boyfriend are oppressed and ultimately killed by the evil chief of police. Instead of the law directing us upwards towards our better, ideal selves, now it is seen as simply evil.

Regarding the rise of the middle classes and developments in opera plots during the eighteenth century, Weaver noted that:

> The conversion of the private performances of opera in private theaters into performances before a paying audience, even if the control of the theater remained in the hands of noblemen, made it a financial necessity to respond to the tastes and demands of an ever-widening public. The change accounts for the many protestations by opera librettists that they were obliged to satisfy the low taste of the audience. The effects of these sociopolitical changes upon opera, as the first of the major [musical] forms to become popular, is apparent and has been often noted.[2]

As politics became democratized, opera, like the plastic arts, became vulgarized.

Between 1890 and 1910 Richard Wagner was the most popular opera composer in Europe. But starting during the early 1930s and through the War and to today, Wagner was surpassed in popularity by the lower-level music of Verdi, Puccini, Mozart and Lortzing. This occurred throughout Europe and even in Germany.[3] This is stunning, considering the promotion of Wagner's music by the Nazis as part of their propaganda. Appeals to the people, even by the National Socialists, so eroded notions of the power of the mind that it lessened the popularity of Wag-

---

[2]Robert L Weaver, "The Consolidation of the Main Elements of the Orchestra: 1470-1768." *The Orchestra*, Joan Peyser, Ed. (Milwaukee: Hal Leonard, 2006), 33.

[3]Ulrick Muller and Peter Wapnewski, *Wagner Handbook* (Cambridge MA: Harvard University, 1992).

ner's higher-level music. (Wagner once quipped that "the people" make a better concept than reality. In general he thought that they were brutes, and they are the model for the crude characters of the giants in the *Ring*.) The unconfined people collapsed into themselves and into the lower-level music of Verdi and Puccini.

When Poland rose up in rebellion against their Russian rulers during the mid nineteenth century, Polish patriots called Poland the "Christ of Nations." In a movie version of *Les Miserables* (1998), a poor, working class woman is fired from her job because she has a child out of wedlock. Because of her poverty and abuse, she succumbs to tuberculosis and dies. She suffers for the sins of society or the narrow-minded values of the manager who fired her. He ultimately feels guilty over her death, repents, adopts the woman's child, and raises it as his own. In all of these examples from opera and film, there is an adversarial relationship with the lower class being righteous, victimized, aggressive and using their will to seek dominance and to realize divine "justice" that is unconfined or unlimited.

A history professor recently observed the profound influence of political correctness in academia:

> No history textbook can today pass muster unless it highlights the insignificant, reduces absolutes to local accident, and eliminates grand narratives in favor of a collection of tales, full of sound and fury, whose chief goal is to elicit pity, sympathy or guilt.[4]

Only unique and unconfined details and emotion count today. As the Catholics have books of martyrology, academic works today are books of victimology. Opera singer Eileen Farrell released a recording called "I've Got a *Right* to Sing the

---

[4] Allen Guelzo, "Hero, Standing." *Imprimis*, May/June, 2009. Volume 38, Number 5/6, page 4. Reprinted by permission from *Imprimis*, a publication of Hillsdale College.

Blues" [emphasis added]. In this title, we see the union of natural rights, suffering emotion of the individual, and cathartic aesthetics. Modernists have reduced the West to a collection of blubbering idiots.

Around 1915, expressionist artist Egon Schiele was convicted of creating child pornography. After release from prison, he made a drawing of himself as St. Sebastian. In most Old Master paintings of this subject, the Saint is standing firm as arrows pierce his body. In Schiele's version, his body is convulsing with pain as he takes the arrows. In other words, he had a right to sing the blues. He suffers for the sins of society. As Christian martyrs were Christ-types, so is Schiele and everyone else today.

The history of the word "society" needs a closer examination at this point. It has changed meaning significantly during the last two centuries. At the beginning of the nineteenth century, as seen in the novels of Jane Austin, it meant the upper class and their social life, as in the best society or *beau monde*. When Greta Garbo was starting her career, a friend introduced her into "smart society."[5] This image of the upper class as smart or superior is the traditional Platonic conception. In contrast, Durgnat described one of Garbo's co-stars, John Gilbert, as "scatterbrained." This is how Plato would have described the lower class.

By the 1960s the term *society* had morphed into a negative and evil force that infects and corrupts people, in social conditioning from groups, institutions and norms. This displacement of evil was easy to do because of the connection in the mind between self and body imagery or the collective. If the unrestrained individual was no longer evil, then society was the next best candidate because of the fluid connection. For instance, in a California high school, if a student misbehaves, it is the teacher's fault. Administrators presume that the students are

---

[5]Raymond Durgnat and John Kobal, *Greta Garbo* (New York: E. P. Dutton., 1967).

good kids and the teacher is responsible for maintaining class order. In this situation, society is bad.

Rousseau described this new concept in the eighteenth century. He argued that people are born good but are corrupted by society. As we have seen in the operas, the nineteenth century was a transitional age when the upper class was viewed as evil and hostile but not responsible for creating the personalities of the public at large. This moral perspective is also an inversion of Plato, because for him the upper class were good and wise, and a source of confining control on the evil of the lower class, who were traditionally viewed as the criminal class. (Sociologist James Henslin reported that today in the United States, 90 percent of homicide offenders are lower class.[6])

Early nineteenth century conservative Joseph de Mestra believed that religious observance and social hierarchy were necessary to control evil or crime. Today modernists believe the opposite: that the lower class and its representatives in government must control the upper class or the evils of big business. This creates the evil image of the nineteenth century robber baron and money bags. Instead of the lower class being "robbers" and murderers now it is the upper class. The word *villain* derives from the French word for the lower classes.

Gradually over the past two centuries, evil was displaced from the body, from sexuality, and from the lower class, to the upper class, their art and proper morals or etiquette. Also, during this time the positive qualities of the upper class, such as being smart, worthy and beautiful were moved down to the lower classes. During the mid-nineteenth century, a movement called "The Young Germans" arose, and one of their beliefs was sexual liberation. Wagner belonged to this group. Moreover, by 1900 there started to be more sexual imagery in public.

By the 1920s and '30s in Hollywood film, sensuality was more accepted than it would have been fifty years earlier. A

---

[6]James Henslin, *Social Problems* (Englewood Cliffs NJ: Prentice-Hall, 1990).

colleague of Greta Garbo said that Garbo didn't think that sex was evil.[7] Garbo came from the lower class. In the film *Love* (1927) based on the novel *Anna Karenina*, actors John Gilbert and Greta Garbo play a couple in an adulterous affair. The woman proposes that they keep it a secret. The man responds by saying, "We can't go around acting as if our love is scandalous." So their love is righteous. The body is righteous. Off the set, John Gilbert used to brag, even to studio executives, that his mother was a prostitute. Attitudes were definitely changing.

The displacement of evil, via the connection in the mind between self and group, collected the notions and metaphors previously linked to the body, to the lower class, and to nature. It shifted them upwards through Platonic hierarchy to the form-creating faculty of the mind-to the upper class, and their art. Suddenly the traditional forms, instead of being viewed as liberating, were viewed as confining and oppressive. The elements of nature and the body that were formerly low, confining, cluttered, claustrophobic and evil became high and good. Sex and the body became beautiful and the lower class became smart or worthy, as upper-class society had once been viewed. Conversely, sexual repression became evil and something itself to be repressed as we can see in the male character's comment about his affair in the movie *Love*.

Social controls on behavior and their upper-class and religious proponents came to be seen as claustrophobic pollution, instead of the body and emotion themselves. Virtue became mere dark-age clutter or confinements to be swept away. Again, the transference was eased by the connection between felt emotion of the individual and the emotions of the large vocabulary of body images in the unconscious or dreams. So social forms of repression became evil, and the individual became good or beautiful instead of the reverse, which had been the case for centuries

---

[7]Mark A Vieira, *Irving Thalberg: Boy Wonder to Producer Prince* (Berkeley CA: University of California, 2010).

As divinity once came down from the king to the people, so did all the good or ideal characteristics of the upper class. The lower class became, as we have seen, smart or wise, dominant, and thus worthy to be listened to, as the lower classes used to listen to the upper in earlier centuries. So, not only did perception of evil move upwards, but perception of good moved downwards. In the *Commedia dell'Arte* or Italian street theater of the eighteenth century, aristocrats and professionals were portrayed as fools, while the lower class were portrayed as wise. This is evident in Mozart's opera *Don Giovanni*, which portrays the Don as ruthless and without conscience, while his servant is portrayed as conscientious. One historian said that the Enlightenment had an idealized everyman, and this was in part the basis for the French Revolution. A painting by Edward Manet of a beggar, from about 1870, hangs in the Norton Simon Museum in California. The commentary to the painting says that at that time people believed that the poor had special wisdom. Of course, this is often implied in *Les Miserables*. This helps to explain the hyperbole cited earlier when fast food chains and television advertisements describe average people.

That the upper class is viewed as evil and mindless today is clear in films such as *Titanic*. The upper class is explicitly described as mindless while a lower-class character is portrayed as full of wisdom. Over the last thousand years the theocracy of the Middle Ages was replaced by divine-right monarchy, which in turn was replaced by divine-right individualism. With the decline of the church and aristocracy came a rise by the nineteenth century in secular heroes such as Beethoven, Goethe, Liszt, and the industrialists and inventors. The Romantic artists believed in a cult of individual emotional expression and style.

One important way that we connect with other people is through the mind and its images and concepts of other people. This is evident in anthropomorphism. We not only move from self to others through the connection, but also from group to self through resonance, as we saw in the discussion of homosexuals in the first chapter and the pressure they feel and often adapt to. If the individual was not to be seen as evil, then the group and its norms was the next best candidate. It is an easy transition. The individual's vision of heterosexuality and its image in the mind, as we saw in dreams, are examples of confining, evil society that must be overthrown for modernism. The curse of modernism is not mere liberalism. Not just the left believes in it. It is something to which even many Republicans are sympathetic. What motivates modernists of every ideology is the vision of triumphant individualism. This is even apparent among libertarians and objectivists, or the followers of Ayn Rand.

"Tax the Rich!" is a rebellious impulse. As Christians had the confining evil and suffering of our bodies thrust upon them during the expulsion from the Garden, they now have the confining evil and suffering of society, social conditioning, the upper class, Classical art, and government thrust upon them. This is the source of the abuse excuse common today, and why in the high school described earlier, administrators assume that kids are good, but teachers are bad. "Society" is bad, not people. There is no longer original sin or equivalent. Again, this transference sprang from the fluid connection between self and others or group.

In an episode of *Friends*, a character says, "Monogamy is too cruel a rule" which of course comes from "society" or "out there" or a confinement "from them."

Most modernists of the nineteenth and twentieth century were raised as Christians, so we can see how the traditional notion of Christian freedom morphed into the modernist idea of freedom. For Christians, "freedom" was freedom from the confining or sinful body or evil. We can see how this inspired the aesthetic priorities of Reynolds in viewing nature as confining. For modernists, freedom is freedom from the oppression or evil of the upper class against the heroic and virtuous lower class. Freedom also became freedom from upper-class art forms that became experienced as confining, cluttering and as thrust upon us. As an art critic said about the *Salon* of 1824, "The cry for freedom has been heard by the artists." With a new concept of good and evil came a new definition of freedom, new forces to be fought for and against. Modernism has simply recast the battle between good and evil. To be unconfined is good while to be confined is evil, as we have seen.

Confinement, captivity and claustrophobia, things to be criticized and rebelled against today, are common themes in traditional Christian literature. As theologian John R. W. Stott observed:

> Sin does not only estrange; it enslaves. If it alienates us from God, it also bring us into captivity....
> A university professor describes in his autobiography how he was traveling one day on the top of a bus when "without words and (I think) almost without images, a fact about myself was somehow presented to me. I became aware that I was holding something at bay, or shutting something out or, if you like, that I was wearing some stiff clothing, like corsets, or even a suit of armor, as if I were a lobster."[8]

Traditional Christians had impulses to rebel against and control their bodies' enslaving, confining evil. They aspired to the unlimited in God. In contrast, during the nineteenth century the lower classes, liberal intellectuals, and avant-garde artists had impulses to rebel against the social control of the evil upper classes and their art and government. The finer elements were now experienced as thrust upon them, confining and enslaving. People started to aspire to the unlimited in themselves. This became the righteous and pure battle for freedom. People were tired of feeling confined and of all the impure clutter. Richard Wagner was opposed to laws, contracts and marriage, and instead believed that free love could unite people. As traditional Christians felt "hemmed in" or enslaved

---

[8]John R. W. Stott, /em Basic Christianity (London: Inter-Varsity Press, 1971), 75, 128.

by the fallen body, and wanted elevation and freedom, now modernism felt hemmed in and enslaved by confining social hierarchy and beauty in art, and want elevation, purification, destruction or revolution. During the late nineteenth century, in the Henry James novel The American, a character describes the experience of attending a ball in Paris in these terms: "I felt as if I were walking up and down in the armoury, in the Tower of London!"[9] He felt trapped like a lobster. Similarly, Plato described the ethereal soul as trapped in the prison-like body, and this inspired the Christian interpretation of "the fall" from grace and transcendence in Genesis. In *Les Miserables*, a convicted, lower class criminal is described:

> Through the diseased perceptions of an incomplete nature and a smothered intelligence, he vaguely felt that a monstrous *weight* was over him [emphasis added]. In that pallid and sullen shadow which he crawled, wherever he turned his head and endeavored to raise his eyes, he saw, with mingled rage and terror, forming, massing, and mounting up out of view above him with horrid escarpments, a kind of frightful accumulation of things, of laws, of prejudices, of men, and of acts, the outlines of which escaped him, the weight of which appalled him, and which was no other than that prodigious pyramid that we call civilization. Here and there in that shapeless and crawling mass, sometimes near at hand, sometimes afar off, and upon inaccessible heights, he distinguished some group, some detail vividly clear, here the jailer with his staff, here the gendarme [police officer] with his sword, yonder the mitered archbishop; and on high, is a sort of blaze of glory, the emperor crowned and resplendent. It seemed to him that these distant splendors,

---

[9]Henry James, *The American* (New York: Signet Classics, 1872/1965), 339.

far from dissipating his night, made it blacker and more deathly. All this, laws, prejudices, acts, men, things, went and came above him, according to the complicated and mysterious movement that God impresses upon civilization marching over him and crushing him with an indescribably tranquil cruelty and inexorable indifference. Souls sunk to the bottom of possible misfortune, and unfortunate men lost in the lowest depths, where they are no longer seen, the rejected of the laws, feel upon their heads the whole weight of that human society, so formidable to him who is without it, so terrible to him who is beneath it.[10]

A music historian said that Arnold Schoenberg developed his atonal system of music to "get rid of the underbrush of tonal harmony."[11] Similarly, a dance historian wrote that the nineteenth century choreographer Marius Petipa "was over seventy two; he had great experience, but was weighed down by cliques and stereotyped methods of production."[12] Dance was purified by subsequent attacks from the modernists. Recall here how everyone feels social pressure or weight because of the connection in the mind. In the opera *Andrea Chenier* (1895) which takes place in Paris during the Revolution, Maddalena says, "Suffering, dying in a bodice, heavy as armor, a man would not want to wear, or in a corset they promised would not harm her, ridiculous convention!" (act one). In an episode of *Sex and the City*, Carrie Bradshaw is trying on a wedding dress, and she suddenly sits on the floor, and cries, "I'm suffocating! I'm suffocating!" and in desperation removes the dress. We have all heard repeatedly from feminists how oppressive marriage is for women and

[10]Victor Hugo, Charles E. Wilbour, trans., *Les Miserables* (New York: Modern Library, 1992), 80.

[11]Robert Greenberg, *How to Listen to and Understand Great Music*, 3rd Edition, DVD lecture series (Chantilly VA: The Teaching Company, 2006).

[12]Natalia Roslavleva, *Era of the Russian Ballet* (London: Victor Gollancz, 1966), 134.

worthy of attack or purification. It is simply confining clutter to be brushed aside or purified.

We should all simply love one another, as Wagner and the hippies think. There is purity and redemption in love. In another episode, Bradshaw put it succinctly: "marriage plus baby equals death." As sin equaled entrapment and death, so now does marriage and class, society, social pressure, or confinement. The problem today is not seen as pressure from base nature and the body, but social pressure felt in the mind.

One way that dominant male chimpanzees express their rank is by jumping, leapfrog fashion, over lower ranking apes.[13] Dominant apes often express their rank by being literally higher than the others.   Such strategy or confining oppression is evident in human behavior. Royalty are sometimes referred to as "Highness" and they "ascend" to the throne. In an episode of *Friends*, Phoebe, Ms New Age, contests the idea of evolution. Another character compares the certainty of evolution with gravity, and Phoebe responds by saying, "I feel less pulled than pushed" and then she bent her body at the hip. As the dominant chimp presses down to show his dominance, now science and the upper classes are seen as pressing down or oppressing as we saw with Hugo and his pyramid of civilization or group pressure. People need to criticize this confinement, throw it off and be purified to be liberated, real, whole and unlimited. To legally enforce heterosexuality as in the nineteenth century would be a confining and oppressive sin.

This perspective is reflected in a recent set design for a production of the ballet *Swan Lake*. In the first act set, a large wall represents the oppression that prince Siegfried feels; "he's trapped," according to designer Jonathan Fensom. Similarly, after looking at a piece of ornate eighteenth century French furniture, a woman commented that it "makes me feel claustrophobic" or confined. And an art historian said that a similar piece of

---

[13]Frans De Waal, *Chimpanzee Politics*, 25th Anniversary Edition (Baltimore: Johns Hopkins University, 2007).

furniture suffered from "suffocating luxury", and another piece
he described as "vulgar,"[14] as nature was vulgar for Winckelmann, as quoted earlier. Ornament, as a product of imposing
society, is viewed as needing to be purified or purged, is sinful,
and thus it is viewed as a confining "crime" according to architect Adolph Loos. It is pollution and clutter to be purged, as the
lower aspects of the body used to be viewed as pollution to be
purged.

The film *Guess Who's Coming to Dinner* (1967) is about the
reaction of a pair of Black parents, and a pair of White parents
to the proposed marriage of a Black man and a White woman.
The White father objects to the marriage, and a priest tries to
discourage this reaction by saying, "You're not going to make
heavy weather of this?" The Black father also opposes the marriage, and his son attacks him by calling him and his beliefs
"dead weight." Traditional views on "race" and miscegenation
have become oppressive and confining weight or pollution. It
offers no vision of the unlimited. Since traditional notions of
"race" resulted from attitudes and laws promoted and instituted
by Westerners, so Western culture is now seen as pressing down.
It is pollution, according to the new perspective or new definition of confinement. From modernist perspective, we must
purge ourselves of impure, limiting Western Culture.

An art historian of the 1950s felt that the term *purity* was
appropriate when discussing changes made to Baroque architecture. He observed that, "The present facade of S. Andrea Della
Valle, therefore, is a High Baroque alteration of a Maderno design by Carlo Rainaldi, whose design in its turn was "purified"
and stripped of its ambiguities by Carlo Fontana."[15] The context
is different from a discussion of modernism versus classicism,
but the modernist impulse made it seem obvious to use the word
in this other context.

---

[14]Richard Bretell, *Museum Masterpieces: The Metropolitan Museum of
Art*, DVD lecture series (Chantilly VA: The Teaching Company, 2007).

[15]Rudolf Wittkower, *Art and Architecture in Italy 1600-1750: II. High
Baroque* (New Haven: Yale University, 1999), 104.

The feelings of imposition that we see among Christians and modernism result from the input or pressure from sinful or confining "group body" imagery. People feel stimulation or pressure from bodies and body imagery, as we saw in the first chapter, and this is evident in the idea of having our bodies thrust upon us by God in Genesis. Traditionally this stimulation was seen as impure "temptation." That word is largely gone from the culture, but it was powerful before about 1960.

The professor quoted above was keeping something at bay, or felt enslaved or hemmed in like a lobster because he was rebelling against the stimulation of his impure body, the sinful stimulation or temptation coming in from impure body imagery. This would result in stimulation or confining and impure debasement. Obviously, he got the idea and feelings from Genesis and Plato. We also see this with modernism; Hugo's character felt enslaved or hemmed in by confining, impure civilization because of the pressure of perceived class hierarchy or impure, artificial society that comes in his senses through other bodies and especially the upper class. As the professor revolted against the sinful feelings of impure stimulation, Hugo's character rebelled against the confining and impure feelings of being at the bottom of the class hierarchy, or of having this thrust upon him resulting in his "smothered intelligence." His crushing debasement clearly resulted from society and not his own nature.

Today, not just the lower classes, but almost everyone, on both the left and right, rebel against confining, cluttering and impure society. Only the most conservative support confining nationalism. As the professor felt "oppressed" and enslaved by the impure, and desired to keep something out, so does Hugo and so do most people today.

Perception and differentiation between self and group or body imagery are essential steps. Bodies and class markers, like clothing, stimulate everyone. The fundamental factor is, "Do we have feelings of acceptance or rebellion against the confining and the 'impure'?" Before the eighteenth century most people accepted hierarchy, but then they started to have feelings of re-

bellion, as modern homosexuals rebel against the confining and
impure norms of their official body imagery, instead of fitting in
as they do in most parts of the world and in most of history. As
homosexuals once fit in, people once fit into their place in the
great chain of being.

One female college administrator said, "Chaos is good."
Victor Hugo describes the importance of the irregular:

> Until now all that [police officer Javert] had above
> him had been in his sight a smooth, simple, limpid
> surface; nothing there unknown, nothing obscure;
> nothing which was not definite, co-ordinated, con-
> catenated, precise, exact, circumscribed, limited,
> shut in, all foreseen; authority was a plane; no fall
> in it, no dizziness before it. Javert had never seen
> the unknown except below. The irregular, the unex-
> pected, the disorderly opening of chaos, the possi-
> ble slipping into an abyss; that belonged to inferior
> regions, to the rebellious, the wicked, the miser-
> able. Now Javert was thrown over backward, and
> he was abruptly startled by this monstrous appari-
> tion; a gulf on high.[16]

Both of these terms, the *irregular* and the *unexpected*, figure
large in our assessment of modernism. We hear them regularly
from the mouths of modernists themselves. One psychologist
said that fantasies can be more powerful than reality. The terms
of our social relations are largely determined by psychology and
philosophy.

As traditional Christians had feelings or fantasies of
rebellion against the enslaving stimulation from confining and
impure body imagery, temptation, and sought the regularities
of Godly virtue, now people have fantasies of rebelling with
Godly, perfect irregularities against impure social hierarchy,

---

[16]Victor Hugo, Charles E. Wilbour, trans., *Les Miserables* (New York:
Modern Library, 1992), 1144.

the norm or society. There is nothing worse today then being a dupe of society, of class, gender etc., as there once was nothing worse than being a dupe of the body or the devil. Both resulted in impure false consciousness and moral collapse. As the ideal once was to rise above or transcend the impure body by adhering to the group, now the ideal is to break or rise above impure society, the impurities of confining class, gender and "race" through the assertion of subversive irregularities. One woman said, "I became a lesbian for political reasons." This impulse gives modernists their aloof righteousness and the desire to attack the advocates of impure society. A woman threw a cup of water in the face of biologist Edward O. Wilson during a lecture because in his books he reveals bio-determinism. A Columbia professor proposed that all research into human variation should be outlawed. The aloof and disdainful attitude today is "You're not going to tempt me with confining notions of class, gender or race," as Christians were not to be tempted by the sinful body. As Western culture was once above the body, now modernists are above the social body. As Westerners once made jokes and laughed at the body, now they make jokes and are dismissive of society. Only a dark-age religion such as modernism could inspire such dark-age attitudes and behavior as attacking science.

This explains the popularity of relativism and particularism among the young. It is a strategy to suppress the evil social body-pressure from the stratified group and the mind. That an individual's nature comes from out there makes perfect sense given the connection that exists in the mind; but also because the confining and stratified group is evil or alien, it also makes sense to attack and suppress it as something outside, as we once did the body. As the body was contagious, now the social body is. "Everything is relative" and if not, then you are damned. It is true that human behavior can be changed, but not human nature nor its hierarchical aspect and dynamics of body imagery. We have more limited options than is generally believed.

The new use of the word "vulgar" as we saw above in the

discussion of art is an example of the displacement of our traditional ideas about the body and nature onto confining, imposing, excessive and impure high art. Similarly, regarding French
Neoclassicism, Bordes notes:

> During the Consulate and Empire, the number of
> publications reproducing vases attests to a novel
> *vulgarization* of antiquarian knowledge and a new
> appreciation for the naivete of these models [em-
> phasis added].[17]

As it was once naive and vulgar to fall for the body, now
it is said to be naive and vulgar to fall for society. Similarly,
Regis Michel notes: "Here Greece is just an empty form. A
pure formalism-or rather: a fetishism."[18] As the body was once
illusion or empty form, so now is classicism. Modernists believe that the social body is mere imposition, vulgar, impure,
and fetishistic, as the body was once impure and fetishistic. The
social body is seen today as the confining and disgusting condition of injustice to be criticized, overthrown or purified. "All
art forms are equal!" is a common piece of wisdom today as
part of a strategy to suppress the social body. Again, we see the
resulting transference of metaphors from the body and nature to
the government, upper-class norms, and the Classical tradition.
During the 1920s, the avant-garde referred to the nineteenth
century as "The bad nineteenth century," or unjust. Clothing
fashion by this time started to show the natural contours of the
body as people threw off the enslaving, polluting, and impure
oppression of finely patterned and formed clothing styles.

The inversion of Platonism appears in other areas of life.
Arthur Lovejoy was a philosophy professor at Johns Hopkins
University for about 20 years, and he is the founder of the dis-
cipline of intellectual history. In *The Great Chain of Being*, he

---

[17]Philippe Bordes, *Jacques-Louis David: Empire to Exile* (New Haven:
Yale University, 2005).

[18]Regis Michel, *Le beau ideal ou l'art du concept* (Paris, 1989), 127 trans-
lated in Bordes (2005), 275.

describes how by the early nineteenth century, developments in theology and science were motivated by an inversion of Platonism. Harvard published this book in 1936. It has been in print ever since and is considered a classic.

During the nineteenth century, the triumph of good over evil resulted in redemption. The battle today is transformed by modernism. People achieve redemption by attacking the evil or impure upper classes and the Classical tradition. Adolf Loos, an early modernist architect, sought redemption from historical styles.[19] Seeking redemption through art was a common idea during the nineteenth century, and was adhered to by Chopin and Wagner.

Academic departments today brook no contradictions, disrespect, or lack of love from students when it comes to modern art theory or aesthetics. As looking at a Byzantine icon should inspire love from votaries, looking at modern art should inspire love from its votaries. If you love modern art, then you are redeemed or good, while if you do not love it, then you are unredeemed, a heretic, or evil. If loving modern art is necessary to graduate, then who would want to commit the crime of loving ornament and real beauty? It would resemble worshiping the devil, the very vision of the regular as we saw in Hugo's description. In Act One of the opera *Andrea Chenier* (1895), which takes place during the French Revolution, Gerard says:

> Gilded palace, I loathe you! The image of a vain
> world besotted with *corruption* [emphasis added]!
> Dainty gallants in silks, bedecked with treasures,
> dance your dances, and enjoy your minuets. Your
> graceful gavottes and useless measures! Your fate
> is sealed, I warn you! Frivolous race, and *vile* [emphasis added]!

His moral perspective on beauty and its proponents is that

---

[19]Carl E. Schorske, *Fin-De-Siecle Vienna: Politics and Culture* (New York: Vintage Books, 1981).

of most modernists. It is nothing but frivolous or impure clutter to be swept away.

One modern art critic sensed the connection between modern art, or at least Picasso and religion:

> Picasso's great painting *Demoiselles d'Avignon* is a kind of vital revolt against a Classical tradition of which Ingres was the leading symbol and which fascinated Picasso: a tradition he had at once to smash to pieces and reinvent. This is what his *Demoiselles* do, chopping up the old classicism with an axe and parading over the ruins in all their barbarous sexual power. Picasso's painting-a brothel scene-shattered the canon at the heart of Classical since ancient times and "savagely" desacralizes the human figure. Yet at the same time, in drenching that figure in the vitality of non-European traditions-as if in the blood of some pagan sacrifice-he gives it a new sacred dimension. No question: it was at the cost of this destruction that Picasso was regularly able to revive the great Mediterranean tradition and provide humanity with radiant myths.[20]

We saw earlier how important sexual liberation and the redemption of the body were for the formation of modernist ethics. Now we see again, how those ethics are expressed aesthetically. Although Picasso does not use explicit religious images, it was still clear to the writer that Picasso was working within a mythic context for the creation of his modern art which smashes to destroy, redeem, and be reborn. Instead of the heroic being employed for self-control, and for maintaining art that inspired self-control, the heroic is now used to attack the norm of self-control.

---

[20]Manuel Jover, *Ingres* (Paris: Terrail/Edigroup, 2005), 247.

In response to the feelings of infringement from classicism, people have developed several ways of redeeming and purifying rebellion. They consist of expressing and romanticizing the emotions, and doing anything stylistically and ideologically to attack the Classical tradition and elevated social controls in general. Contrasting modern art with the Rococo painting of Boucher, Hyde and Ledbury observed that:

> The persuasive power of the modern (ist) aesthetic-of a self-critical, *pure*, anti-theatrical, autonomous, and, above all, "deep" and serious minded painting that operates in a realm far remote from that of decoration, or even representation, and must exist in a certain antagonism with patronage-may be too great for Boucher's painting to withstand [emphasis added].[21]

Notice that one of the first things the authors reported is "purity." One Marxist during the 1920s was explicit:

> In the name of our To-morrow we will burn Rafael, destroy museums, crush the flowers of art. Maidens in the radiant kingdom of the Future will be more beautiful than Venus de Milo.[22]

A few years ago French conductor and composer Pierre Boulez wrote that the opera houses should be burned down or purified. People once burned witches to purify or save them. The objective of one modern artist is to provoke moral outrage.[23]

---

[21] Melissa Hyde and Mark Ledbury, *Rethinking Boucher* (Los Angeles: Getty, 2006), 2.

[22] Lothrop Stoddard, *The Revolt Against Civilization* (New York: Charles Scribner's Sons, 1923), 202.

[23] Ulrick Muller and Peter Wapnewski, *Wagner Handbook* (Cambridge MA: Harvard University, 1992).

As we saw in chapter one, moderation or control is the basis of classicism, with a balance between the body and control or form. For modernism, it is extremism and the unlimited that is loved, allowing as it does the body and irregularities to be fully expressed. Moderation is viewed as boring or an impure imposition as we see with the stigma against sexual repression. So in San Francisco there is a restaurant chain called "Extreme Pizza," and in Edmonton, Alberta, there is a restaurant called "Extreme Pita," and a San Francisco bank had as its slogan "Extreme Banking." As God was unlimited, so now are people and they resist impure limitations or confinements. Nineteenth-century writer E.T.A. Hoffman said that Beethoven's Fifth Symphony was "unlimited." Today, "no limits" is a popular phrase with advertisers. For instance, a recent billboard carried the phrase, "No Dentures; No limits."

Classicists emphasize limits on behavior and intelligence, and the need for social control on native inclinations to evil, hostility, or crime. Modernists, in contrast, experience limits as claustrophobic imposition from the group. So they rebel against anything limiting, such as conceptions of class, sex, "race" and native intelligence that press down on people, pollute with impurities and thus should be attacked with irregularities. Hugo goes so far as to say that limitations create criminal impulses.

This is the source of today's fear of any suggestion of biological determinism. It is equated to the Nazis (the poster boys for evil). Modernist dogma is that human nature's imperfections come from society, not from within. The social body's impulses toward differentiation and discrimination are evil. Modernists strive to purge the social body, not the physical body. A recent study has found that eugenics is popular among professionals in Israel, but out of fashion in Germany.[24]

Wieland Wagner is the grandson of Richard Wagner, and was director of the Bayreuth opera festival during the 1950s.

---

[24] Yael Hashiloni-Dolev, *A Life (Un) Worthy of Living: Reproductive Genetics in Israel and Germany* (Dordrecht, The Netherlands: Springer, 2010).

He said that his productions were "an adventure in the quest for an unknown goal."[25] Whatever results would be unexpected or irregular, and this is the point. Kevin McKenzie, Artistic Director of American Ballet Theater, said in print:

> In a world where you can preorder entertainment-comedy, romance, adventure-an evening at the ballet takes you someplace that's unpredictable. Even if you've seen that particular ballet before, it will be different each time, because of the human element. You may be impressed with the dancers' *athleticism* or with the work's theatrical energy, but in any case your assumption will be *challenged* [emphases added]. That's why we go to live performances.[26]

Notice that he not once mentioned beauty. The motto of Idaho Dance Theater is "Experience the Unexpected." Anything to undermine the norm. They featured on a dance program a piece called "Body Works." The liner notes to a recent recording of Chopin's piano music has the title, "Lord of misrule: Chopin the rebel" and starts with the following sentence, "The whole of Chopin's piano output might well be published under Roald Dahl's title, *Tales of the Unexpected.*[27] Similarly, an art magazine is called *Juxtapose.* A recent newspaper article, in the "Life" section, on a TV documentary about the body, had a picture of several children wearing White T-shirts, and on each shirt was written in a large font one word such as, "VOMIT," "EAR WAX," "SWEAT," "MUCUS," "PUS," and "TEARS."[28] Modernists see this as purity incarnate.

---

[25]Fredrick Spotts, *Bayreuth: A History of the Wagner Festival* (New Haven: Yale University, 1994), 228.

[26]Kevin McKenzie, "Bringing Magic to Center Stage: The Art of American Ballet Theater," in Nancy Ellison, ed., *Classic Style: The Splendor of American Ballet Theater* (New York: Rizzoli International, 2008), 7.

[27]Roger Nichols, "Lord of misrule: Chopin the rebel," Liner notes for CD entitled, *Chopin*, pianist Simon Trpceski (European Union: EMI Records, 2007), 3.

[28]Staff Writer, *Idaho Statesmen*, February 15, 2010, C1.

An announcer for a show distributed by Public Radio International read a published poem that included the phrase "beautiful vulgarity." As beauty was a vision of purity, now vulgarity is a vision of purity. Similarly, Stoddard noted:

> [Regarding] Tolstoy's instinctive aversion to civilization and love of the primitive, "if a stone lies on top of another in a desert, that is excellent. If the stone has been placed upon the other by the hand of man, that is not so good. But if stones have been placed upon each other and fixed there with mortar or iron, that is evil; that means construction, whether it be a castle, a barracks, a prison, a customs-house, a hospital, a slaughter-house, a church, a public building, or a school. All that is built is bad, or at least suspect." The first wild impulse which Tolstoy felt when he saw a building, or any complex whole, created by the hand of man, was to simplify, to level, to crush, to destroy, so that no stone might be left upon the other and the place might again become wild and simple and purified from the work of man's hand. Nature is to him the pure and simple; civilization and culture represent complication and impurity. To return to nature means to expel impurity, to simplify what is complex, to destroy culture.[29]

Tolstoy, in *Anna Karenina*, uses an image of entrapment to describe Anna: "At once thoughts of her home, her husband, her son, and the cares of the coming day and those to follow *surrounded her* [emphasis added]."[30] Tolstoy and Anna felt trapped.

---

[29]Lothrop Stoddard, *The Revolt Against Civilization* (New York: Charles Scribner's Sons, 1923), 132.

[30]Leo Tolstoy, *Anna Karenina*, Richard Pevear and Larissa Volokhonsky, trans. (New York: Penguin, 1877/2000), 103.

What Tolstoy is expressing in the extreme is the reverse of the Classical view of the relationship between nature and civilization or urban constructs. During antiquity, the city was seen as a haven from the barbarism and violence of nature. This is clearly seen in that the Polis or city-state was the preferred mode of life. In the Greek view, the worst condition for a man was to be hearthless and stateless. The wanderings of Odysseus are the best example of this in myth from the period. Aristotle goes so far as to define Man as the "political animal." And Roman myth is very focused on Aeneas and his heroic efforts to found the city of Rome.

This perspective or dichotomy dominated until the eighteenth century, when it started to become inverted. Suddenly cities were seen as corrupting, and nature as pure and innocent and conducive to virtue. There was an inversion of good and evil. This is clear in the writings of Rousseau and Jefferson, and came to define Romantic ideology, and now dominates the West. (After Voltaire read Rousseau, he said something like, "I don't think I can support this, after all I have not been down on all fours since I was a baby.") As we have seen, with natural rights came an empowering of the lower orders, and by association in the Platonic psychology the appetites, and so nature more generally. During the seventeenth century, people were awed by the aristocracy and high clergy, but no longer, and instead became more self-centered as they lowered their sights. People are now awed by themselves. Because of the connection in the mind, the force of evil that was to be fought against was displaced from the body to the public sphere and was, naturally, to be "purged" as we saw with Tolstoy. (A very clear and popular example of this is the film *Ghost in the Machine*, which will be analyzed in chapter 5.) Confining or oppressive evil also went up to the aristocracy resulting in their gradual, and sometimes rapid, purgation. So no longer was nature viewed as barbaric and something to be escaped, but class, and eventually gender and race. No longer the evil body, but the evils of class, gender and race were to be fought against and purged or "domesticated", brought "under control" or legislated against. People today that strongly support notions of class, gender and race are viewed as evil and "wild" and in need of being broken, reformed or tamed. So instead of notions of class being viewed as a taming influence on people, which was popular before the nineteenth century, it is itself now viewed as deviant. We now see by the Enlightenment and the Romantics a redemption of nature and thus of its exuberant and fun irregularities.

To modernists, the irregularities of nature are the ideal that influences modern art and design. The weight of the irregularities of nature, once viewed as confining and claustrophobic, as we saw in Reynolds, are now viewed as liberating against the limitations of the mind, which once was viewed as facilitating transcendence, liberation, or the unlimited. Aesthetics have been inverted. Form is now considered claustrophobic. Righteous-feeling subversion against form and beauty is the dominant morality and aesthetic today. "Subvert the dominant paradigm!" glares the bumper sticker.

In the Classical tradition, nature is imperfect and requires arrangement or perfection by the mind, as we saw with Plato and Reynolds, while in Romanticism and today, nature and its unexpected irregularities are pure, purifying, and perfect. Those rebellious and purifying irregularities are the model for much modern art and the drive toward particularism and diversity.

In an episode of *Friends*, uptight and controlling Monica is excited to have a Victorian style dollhouse. In response, Phoebe, Ms New Age, builds her own dollhouse, but it is flimsy, crude, irregular, and colored with bright and strident colors. After Phoebe shows off her new doll house to everyone, who are huddled around it, Monica tries to get attention and support by saying, "Look at my china cabinet!" and her friends give a faint "ya", don't really look at it, and then go back to adoring Phoebe's house. Modernists know who is morally and aesthetically righteous here.

In the opening scene of Wagner's opera *Das Rheingold*, the dwarf Alberich is in sexual pursuit of the Rhine maidens, and, in disgust they say that he is a "Dirty old devil" and that he should "stop fouling the air with his curses." In the opera *Tosca*, a priest inspired in part by Jesus says:

> [Certain women] compete with the Madonna and have the stench of the devil.

And Jesus said:

> It is what comes out of a person that makes him unclean. For from the inside, from a person's heart, come the evil ideas which lead him to do immoral things, to rob, kill, commit adultery, be greedy and do all sorts of evil things; deceit, indecency, jealousy, slander, pride and folly-all these evil things come from inside a person, and they defile a man.[31]

These quotations show that during the nineteenth century the body was viewed as the source of impure pollution, and for that matter temptation. Similarly, a film historian describes peoples' reaction during the Depression to the polluting egotism from film stars:

during this period, Americans required their stars to be modest, self-effacing and without pretensions...If the public smelled even a whiff of egotism, snobbery or arrogance in a performer's demeanor, he or she was likely to fall quickly out of favor.[32]

In an episode of *Friends*, Monica, commenting on the smell of a friend of Phoebe, simply says, "The odor" and with a tone of slight disgust. Phoebe responds with a righteous tone by saying that her friend "Will shower when Tibet is free." As the body was once seen as the source of confining pollution or impurity, now society is seen as confining, impure and the source of pollution. China, for pressing down on Tibet, should be attacked as impure. Only spontaneous movement from below is

---

[31] Mark, 7:21-23.
[32] Richard Jewell, *The Golden Age of Cinema: Hollywood 1929-1945* (Malden MA: Blackwell, 2007), 271.

righteous and pure, breaking the norm in the mind by the efforts of an individual or revolutionary group, as we saw with Tolstoy and his attacks against civilization. This is the new purity.

In *Les Miserables* Victor Hugo made a remark similar to Tolstoy's but, in addition, made the connection between revolution and the attack against pollution:

> This danger, imminent perhaps in Europe towards the end of the eighteenth century, was cut short by the French Revolution, that immense act of probity. The French Revolution, which is nothing more nor less than the ideal armed with the sword, started to its feet, and by the very movement, closed the door of evil and opened the door of good. It cleared up the question, promulgated truth, drove away *miasma*, purified the century, crowned the people [emphasis added].[33]

As the French Kings wore crowns and were pure, so now do the "the people" and drive away the impurities or confinement of hierarchy.

This is also reflected in the rise of expressionist art by about 1890, and in the fragmentation of art styles occurring in the 1920s. Expressionist art is irregular and its practitioners and proponents are the first to admit it because of its expressive and assaulting nature. Making art became an expression of pure subjectivity, like writing a letter or declaring an ideology such as Dadaism, Futurism, or Surrealism. Picasso was explicit about the political nature of his art. He said, "Painting is not done to decorate apartments; it is an instrument of war against brutality and darkness."[34] An odd claim, given that he painted deliberate distortion. If we were to go back in time, and ask a Byzantine

---

[33] Victor Hugo, Charles E. Wilbour, trans, *Les Miserables* (New York: Modern Library, 1992), 864.

[34] Ian Chilvers, *The Oxford Dictionary of Art* (New York: Oxford University, 2004), 541.

icon painter why he painted in his style, he would say, "to combat brutality and darkness."

As we saw in the first chapter, there is a moderate, even necessary, role for morality in art, but if it dominates in the way that it does today, and did during the dark ages, then it simply destroys art and turns it into pure ideology or a moral lesson.

An important influence on art was technological development around 1900. Telephones, cars, and motorcycles sped up the pace of life. This increased the sense of freedom. For instance, a man who rode one of the first bicycles said, "The freedom is exhilarating." The heady atmosphere that this created helped promote a sense of rebellion against all the old social and moral restrictions that had existed for centuries.

Resistance to form is apparent in television advertisements today. Phantasmagoria is common. To get the viewers attention, objects change from one form to another, or they crash against one another. The wild play of imagination is emphasized, rather than the solidity of objects or their form, as they were during the 1950s. The emphasis on imagination is common today in popular and academic culture, while form and beauty are largely ignored if not outright stigmatized as encroaching impurities that need to be attacked.

An example of the traditional perspective on form can be seen in the discovery of dance as political art. Ivor Guest noted that:

> The glorification of the prince was the raison d'etre of the Renaissance court festivity, of which the French Ballet de Cour became a supreme example.

Regarding dance at the court of Louis the fourteenth, Guest continues that:

> The focal figure, however, remained the king, who moved with superb elegance and, by personifying some allegorical character such as Apollo or the

Sun King, conveyed the political message of his absolute authority.[35]

We see a parallel today with the absolute authority of the
bestial aspects of the individual expressed in movement. On an
episode of *Friends*, Rachel decides to go running with Phoebe.
When they run, Rachel is embarrassed because Phoebe runs
with her arms and legs flailing around. Rachel tries to make excuses to not run with Phoebe, but Phoebe eventually figures out
that Rachel is embarrassed and reprimands her for being concerned about what other people think instead of being focused
on their friendship. Eventually Rachel is convinced and starts
to share and enjoy Phoebe's hysterical running style. As she is
running with her arms and legs flailing around, she yells, "Look
how graceful I am!" Distortion and hysteria are seen as the new
grace or movement of the sovereign and unlimited individual.
Eruption of the irregular and unexpected also develops in dance
today.

One historian of dance said that it is easier to define what
modern dance is not, than what it is. Any disjointed and cathartic distortion of the body is seen as dance today. This is done in
the name of self-expression, which is seen as pure.

It is common to think today that art is simply a matter of
convention, but according to one former ballerina, ballet is a
science:

> Ballet [was] a system of movement as rigorous and
> complex as any language. Like Latin or ancient
> Greek, it had rules, conjugations, declensions. Its
> laws, moreover, were not arbitrary; they corre-
> sponded to the laws of nature. Getting it "right"
> was not a matter of opinion or taste: ballet was a
> hard science with demonstrable physical facts. It
> was also, and just as appealingly, full of emotions

---

[35]Ivor Guest, *The Paris Opera Ballet* (Alton, UK: Dance Books, 2006),
5-6.

and the feeling that came with music and movement. It was blissfully mute, like reading. Above
all, perhaps, there was the exhilarating sense of
liberation that came when everything worked. If
the coordination and musicality, muscular impulse
and timing were exactly right, the body would take
over. I could let go. But with dancing, letting go
meant everything; mind, body, soul. This is why, I
think, so many dancers describe ballet, for all its
rules and limits, as an escape from the self. Being
free.[36]

So we see here, again, the Classical idea of freedom, and
real fulfillment, through rules. Yes, we can act like animals, as
we saw with Rachel, but this simply results in becoming slaves
to our passions, and our dehumanization. Ballet, with its geometric control, while popular with audiences, is taboo and de-
rided by modernist critics of ballet, who also state that it dehu-
manizes the dancers.[37]

The differences in style between modern dance and ballet
imply different definitions of human nature, regularity, and purity. With ballet, consistent with Plato, humans reach their highest potential by disciplining or literally elevating and purifying
the body with the mind. Female dancers sometimes go on point
to appear as if they are floating and in flight like angels. As with
Renaissance art, a blending of geometry and movement is beautiful, in the Classical sense. Here we have the triumph of the
mind over the vulgar body. With modern dance, what matters is
coming up with some floppy, cathartic and painful-looking series of irregular movements that attacks, overthrows, or purifies
dehumanizing ballet or the mind. Beauty does not matter; what
matters is ideology and embodying the modernist revolt, as we

---

[36] Jennifer Homans, *Apollo's Angels: A History of Ballet* (New York: Random House, 2010).

[37] Janice Ross, *San Francisco Ballet at Seventy-Five* (San Francisco:
Chronicle, 2007).

saw with Rachel.

To modernists, the triumph of this revolt represents the triumph of justice or of the pure, irregular body over the mind. Regarding a performance of early modern dancer Isadora Duncan:

> one witness recalled an entire dance built simply on rising from the floor; it seemed as if the repressed of the world had shed their chains and triumphed over all tyranny.[38]

Hugo could not have put it better.

A sign that modernists are driven by religious righteousness is that it is common for them to call classicists "evil" while classicists simply consider modernists misguided, due to modernists' alleged good intentions.

In Hollywood film during the first half of the twentieth century the romanticizing of realism and emotion became holy writ. A film critic described Eric von Stroheim's film *Greed* (1925):

> If a contest were to be held to determine which has been the filthiest, vilest, most putrid picture in the history of the motion picture business, I am sure that Greed would walk away with the honors. In my seven-year career as a reviewer and in my five-year one as an exhibitor, I do not remember ever having seen a picture in which an attempt was made to pass as entertainment dead rats, sewers, filth, rotten meat, persons with frightful looking teeth, characters picking their noses, people holding bones in their hands and eating like street dogs or gorging on other food like pigs, a hero murdering his wife and then shown with hands dripping with blood.[39]

---

[38] Selma Jeanne Cohen, ed. *Dance as a Theater Art* (Hightstown NJ: Princeton Book Company, 1992), 119.

[39] Mark A. Vieira, *Irving Thalberg: Boy Wonder to Producer Prince* (Berkeley: University of California, 2010), 47.

What a vision of Tolstoy's irregular purity, just like the picture of the children in the White T-shirts mentioned earlier. Regarding the screening of this film, a film critic described how Stroheim:

> Sitting motionless in a straight chair, cane in hand
> and staring right ahead, as if boring through the
> screen, worships realism like an abstract ideal; wor-
> ships it more, and suffers more in its achievement,
> than other men do for wealth or fame.[40]

Modernist ideals were creeping into *popular culture*. In the film *Daddy Long Legs* (1919) a young girl misbehaves, and an adult excuses her by saying that she is just expressing her individuality. In the film *Anna Karenina* (1935), Greta Garbo's character says, "To not think; only to live and feel." There is a similar film called *Theodora Goes Wild* (1936). And the film *Bringing Up Baby* (1938) comprises two people chasing a leopard for over an hour. The *The Philadelphia Story* (1940) romanticizes drunkenness, as we have seen. The 1957 remake of *The Philadelphia Story* is called *High Society*, and the Bacchic figure here is not a drunk, but a man who loves jazz and is sponsoring a jazz festival. The film opens with Louis Armstrong playing his trumpet. The high spirits and strength of Blacks as fantasized by modernists function today as a Bacchic ideal. Modernists experience Blacks today as they experience Niagara Falls, as just a delight.

Around 1930, film star Norma Shearer described her general approach to characters:

> I can't do the Garbo or Dietrich thing. I admire
> them both greatly and wish that I could play such
> characters as they interpret, but I have to go through
> a transition to become worldly. I begin by being

---

[40]Ibid., 46.

> very nice, and then, about the middle of the pic-
> ture, I go *haywire* [emphasis added]. That's when
> things really grow interesting. But if I just stayed
> sweet and appealing, the roles I played would be
> very dull.[41]

Notice the aversion being merely "sweet and appealing."
Recall here the transformation of the West's vocabulary of images as moving from ethnocentric to diverse as described at the
beginning of chapter one. In many films from the period, like
The Awful Truth (1937), women are tempted by rich men, but
they ultimately choose men whom they love. So again we have
the triumph of emotion over impure society.

In recent decades, the trend for expressing the emotions has
gone beyond mere energy and high spirits and has started to be
regularly vulgar in an extreme way as we saw with *Greed*. In
The Sweetest Thing (2002) the female lead walks into a men's
bathroom that is covered with graffiti, lifts up her dress, backs
up to a men's urinal and does her thing. For modernists, this is
the new sweet or pure.

As should be clear, the word *pure* has changed meaning with
the displacement of values that we have outlined. What was low
has now become high, refined, or sweet. In *My Best Friend's
Wedding* (1997), a woman's tongue becomes stuck to the penis
of an ice statue, and the two lead female characters, compete
to make the most noise while snorting. In *There is Something
About Mary* (1998), the male lead masturbates in a bathroom
and the female lead applies his semen to her hair. These exemplify the modern notion of fun and humor.

The inversion of Platonism is the driving force of the plot
to the blockbuster film *Titanic* (1997), which takes place on an
ocean liner in the year 1912. In overview, Rose is a young
woman who is engaged to Cal, a wealthy, overbearing or oppressive man dressed in a tuxedo. She claims to love him, but

---

[41]Mark A. Vieira, *Irving Thalberg: Boy Wonder to Producer Prince*
(Berkeley: University of California, 2010), 186.

expresses throughout the film nothing but contempt and fear of him, of his upper-class friends, and of their confining and impure milieu. In contrast to Cal, fun-loving and down-to-earth Jack is a poorly dressed, penniless artist. He sees Rose in public and falls in love with her. He approaches her, they speak, and she grows to feel the same way. Her growing feelings for him are punctuated with innuendo and declarations that he and his low lifestyle are better than the overly delicate, refined, and polluting lifestyle of her wealthy fianc(e). You definitely get the impression that Cal presses down on people for a living. Jack represents pure nature, while Cal represents polluting culture.

An early scene in the film shows Rose to be a modern woman. She has purchased a Picasso, the painting "Demoiselles d' Avignon," which portrays flat and distorted figures of prostitutes, and comments that "It has truth but no logic." Of course, it is precisely the absence of logic that is the truth of modernism. Notice that they never let illogic get in the way, especially in politics. It would get in the way of purity. In response, Cal shows his true colors by saying, with an arrogant tone, "Picasso, he'll never amount to a thing!" It is clear that he wants to press down on Picasso, and for that matter Rose, and she senses it.

In a later scene, Rose, in disgust, runs away from a party of her rich fianc(e)'s friends, and says to herself, as she is running, that she is sick of their "mindless chatter." It is common for the impurities of the regular and confined to create sickness and so should be attacked and purged. The plot makes clear that the upper class, not the lower, is impure and mindless. She runs to the end of the ship, and is about to commit suicide by jumping off, when Jack sees her and convinces her to not jump. This is the beginning of their bonding. A little later, she shows him her engagement ring, and it is so large that he says, "That would have taken you right to the bottom." Marriage certainly is "heavy" or oppressive, as we saw in *Sex and the City*; it makes one feel bowed over by something dominant and polluting.

Cal and his rich friends learn that Jack saved Rose's life

and in appreciation invite Jack to an elegant dinner complete with parlor music. After the meal, Jack invites Rose to a real party comprised of lower-class people having a good time getting drunk and dancing to folk music. For Plato, mind and its capacity for intelligible control were real while the material world and emotion were incoherent flux. For Jack, and now Rose, the lower classes and their jovial entertainment are real, while the fine manners and art of the upper classes are unreal, fake or impure false consciousness.[42]

As part of Rose's new and improved reality, Jack teaches her how to spit. Her first attempt is timid, but he gives her more robust examples of the fine art of spitting, and she improves. As part of her moral reform, Jack tells Rose that "she is trapped by her rich fianc(e) and lifestyle, and that it is up to her to save herself or else the fire that he loves in her will go out." Notice the word "trapped" as in "confined." By "fire," he is referring to the wild emotion that animates most young people.

As part of their escape from the rich people, Rose and Jack go to the bottom of the ship and have sex in a car. After the sex, she says, "When we dock, I'm getting off with you." He responds, "This is crazy." She says, "It doesn't make any sense: that's why I trust it." Notice the similarity here to her to comment about the Picasso [on page 87]. Except that now she has extended it to include the element of trust. Naturally, one would only trust what has greatest reality. Considering that Jack "pushes up" with irregularities he is pure and real, while Cal "pushes down" and so is impure and fake-overbearing. He is one rock cemented on top of another, and he wants to cement you into place, into your place down on the hierarchy. Modernists see such a confining vision as repulsive or impure.

It becomes clear to Cal and his rich friends that Rose and Jack are in love. Cal becomes angry and confronts Rose. She

---

[42]Editor's note: The publishers are friends with one of the musicians in the Irish session scene. According to him, the film's portrayal of earthy folk as more authentic than the elite was precisely director James Cameron's intent, and the crew worked hard to convey that impression.

becomes even angrier and yells, "I'd rather be his whore than your wife!" then spits in his face. We see clearly the influence of both Toulouse-Lautrec and Picasso during her visit to Paris. This represents the victory of nature over culture. At the end of the film, Rose is portrayed as an old woman. Thinking back on the affair, she says, "He saved me in every way a woman could be saved." As traditionally the lower classes looked to improve themselves by imitating the upper classes, now the upper classes are saved or purified by the irregularities of the lower. Hugo would agree with this. Notice the use of the powerful word *saved* as in "Jesus saved me." He saved her from drowning in both the ocean and the abyss of an upper-class marriage. We see the triumph of the low by the end of the film to the point that it even appropriates Christian images of salvation to this end.

As people had impulses to ascend the divine hierarchy of culture, and be purified and redeemed, now they have impulses to go down and be purified and redeemed. The ballet *La Corsair* is about a girl who is sold into slavery but is rescued by a pirate who becomes her lover. Notice the theme of salvation from enslavement, as in to the traditional idea of sin or a bad state or living condition. Instead of loving Jesus for her salvation, she now loves a pirate. As in *Titanic*, the girl is saved by a low character from enslavement to sin or a bad state. Instead of people looking up for salvation, they now look down.

It is clear that the West is approaching cultural stagnation. A cartoon in *New York* magazine had a picture of a man dressed as a cave man and holding a club. Two women in modern dress are standing next to him and one says to the other, "Joe certainly has become more interesting since he read Camille Paglia." He certainly is a real, stimulating, or beautiful vision. He would make a good modern dancer. He is a prime candidate for attacking impure culture considering that he only has one direction to go in, and that is up against the confining and regular.

In an episode of *Friends*, Chandler says to Joey, "You even cry after Titanic" and Joey responds, almost in tears, "Those two only had each other!" As people during the nineteenth century only had Jesus, now the wretched upper class needs the righteous lower class. Upper-class people smile today when they see lower-class people, instead of finding them disgusting as they did during the nineteenth century. For instance, in the nineteenth century:

> Theatergoers at the upper end of the socioeconomic
> scale became less and less tolerant of what they saw
> as the demonstrative and "uncivilized" behavior of
> the working-class occupants of the gallery seats.[43]

The model so far outlined for modernism and its notion of pollution helps to explain a peculiar early scene in *Titanic*. Jack, a young Italian man, and two Norwegians are playing poker. The Italian and Norwegians have personalities typical of those nations; the Italian has a big, glowing smile, while the Norwegians are tight-lipped and rigid. But one of the Norwegians is inclined to hostility, and at one point becomes so angry that he punches the other Norwegian in the face.

The scene makes no sense relative to the violent crimes rates in Europe during the early twentieth century. At that time, and through the early 1970s, Italy had high homicide rates, while Scandinavia had extremely low rates. It is clear from the data that the more emotionally unrestrained a population, the higher the violent crime rates, while the less emotional populations consistently have lower rates. To put it another way, the more that a population has a generous perspective on the emotions, the more prone to crime they are, or to emotional outbursts. The more constricted a population is, the lower the crime.The fight scene in Titanic goes against type. In reality, the Italian more likely would have punched the Norwegian.

Nevertheless, the scene fits the pattern of logic that we have seen in modernism. If social controls are polluting, and create

---

[43]Robert C. Allen, "The Movies in Vaudeville: Historical Context of the Movies as Popular Entertainment," *The American Film Industry*, Tino Balio, ed. (Madison: University of Wisconsin, 1985), 87.

problems like hostility, as we saw with Hugo, then it makes sense that the tight-lipped Norwegian would be hostile. The body is innocent and good, and social controls on the body are evil. Hence, the Norwegian is portrayed as evil, while the Italian is nice and jovial. His body is innocent or untouched.

Another scene in *Titanic* shows Jack as a Christ-type. Cal frames Jack for a crime and Jack is put in custody by being handcuffed to a pole. Cal oppresses him. One of Cal's henchmen punches Jack in the stomach while he is handcuffed, because of his affair with Rose. This scene is modeled on the flagellation of Christ who was also tied to a pole and flogged.

We analyze this film in detail partly because it is a particularly good example. It is so systematic that it could be described as a modernist Platonic Dialogue or passion play. But also because of the film's popularity. Within a year of its release, in 1997, it was the highest grossing film in history, 1.8 billion, and was not surpassed until Avatar in 2010. It held that title for 13 years. Newspaper articles on the film during its run described how it reduced even men to tears, and how people were so obsessed with this 3 hour film that they saw it repeatedly. It won eleven Academy Awards, including Best Picture.

Its appeal is to the deepest roots of modernism. To place nature or the body and emotion above restraint is probably the easiest thing that people can do, and is probably the norm among primitive tribes and certainly among apes. It is counterintuitive to be rationalistic and cultured or refined, and to be stratified accordingly, as we were from the Renaissance to about 1900. Dualism, the belief that there is a basic difference between the mind and body, may be out of fashion in science and philosophy, but it is alive and thriving in popular modernist culture.

It is worth noting that during the nineteenth century, entertainers were considered low class or disreputable. They were viewed as mere imitators, morally loose and hence low in Plato's hierarchy. Society leveled the criticism of moral looseness on early Hollywood actors, though the studios tried to keep them under control with morality clauses in their contracts. A part of today's inverted culture, they are now the new glamorous aristocracy, replacing the industrialists and inventers of the nineteenth century as objects of fascination and envy.

Consider the concept of *poverty*. Before 10,000 years ago everyone on earth lived as hunter-gathers, and had almost nothing or were poor. Then people discovered the mind, as expressed by the domestication of plants and animals. During the last 3,000 years we have discovered reason and this has allowed us to conquer nature. Some individuals play a larger and more constructive role in this process and so accumulate more money and so rise above poverty. The question is not, "Why is there poverty?" but why have certain groups and subgroups risen above it? Constructing a life style or standard of living above poverty is what requires an explanation. Poverty is natural.

Chopin describes the political mood in early nineteenth century Paris:

> You meet with crowds of beggars with menacing looks on their faces, and you often hear threatening remarks about that imbecile [King] Louis-Philippe.... The lower classes are completely exasperated and ready at any time to break out of their poverty-stricken situation, but unfortunately for them the government is extremely severe on such movements and the slightest gathering in the streets is dispersed by mounted police.[44]

The poor are seen as oppressed, as Anna Karenina was surrounded by her polluting family. The regular pressing down on the irregular is to be lamented as we saw with Hugo. Here, as in Hugo's description of the prisoner, the lower class responds to natural poverty as if it were an artificial, imposed, social condition, are "menacing" with their newly empowered wills, and

---

[44] As quoted in Jeremy Siepman, *Chopin: The Reluctant Romantic* (Boston: Northeastern University, 1995), 83.

that King Louis-Philippe is an "imbecile," as Cal and his friends were "mindless." As part of our inversion of values, the lower classes are now seen as righteous or wise, have power, and are justified to be hostile, while the upper classes are fools, "mindless", who do not deserve to have power, and if they do, they are viewed as hubristic, as we saw with Cal in *Titanic*.

Chapter 4

Chained at the Bottom of the Cave, or the Power of Hierarchy

We think of the peace and love movement as being a recent invention, from the 1960s, but it had supporters in England during the first decades of the twentieth century. The battle at that time was between Winston Churchill, who represented the conservatives, and, representing the peaceniks, what is known as the Bloomsbury group, the most famous members being E.M. Forster, Virginia Wolf and Maynard Keynes. Valiunas, in a recent article, contrasting Churchill and the Bloomsbury group, said:

> If Churchill was for it—ardent patriotism, empire building as moral duty and ordeal, the primacy of public life over private, war as an eternal feature of human existence—Bloomsbury was sure to be against it. Bold iconoclasts and antagonists, the Bloomsberries, as they called themselves with a giggle, promoted peaceable cosmopolitanism and the incomparable sweetness of the private life well lived, the worldly salvation to be found in art and

91

love, comfort and abandon. In Lytton Strachey's words, "a great deal of a great many kinds of love" was the desired apex of civilized living.[1]

Keynes describes the effect on them by the Cambridge professor G. E. Moore:

> Nothing mattered except states of mind, our own and others people's of course, but chiefly our own. These states of mind were not associated with action or achievement or with consequences. They consisted in timeless, passionate states of contemplation and communion, largely unattached to *before* and *after*.... The appropriate subjects of passionate contemplation and communion were a beloved person, beauty and truth, and one's prime objects in life were love, the creation and enjoyment of aesthetic experience and the pursuit of knowledge. Of these love came a long way first.[2]

The Bloomsberries were one of the first to start simply hanging out. They were progressive or looked forward to things to come. Keynes and the other Bloomberries turned Moore's philosophy into a religion-one without morals though they were never explicit about this. The only kind of action they would admit was love. They disdained social action such as politics, success, ambition, or wealth. E.M. Forster, in his essay, "What I Believe" declared his dislike for great men. He believed that:

> They produce a desert of uniformity around them and often a pool of blood too, and I always feel a little man's pleasure when they come a cropper.

---

[1] Algis Valiunas, "Shall We Fight for Kind and Country?" *Claremont Review of Books*, Volume X, Number 1, Winter 2009/10, 50.
[2] Idem.

> One of the best things about democracy is that it
> produces, instead of Great Men, different kinds of
> small men-a much finer achievement.[3]

We see in this quotation two themes that we have seen repeatedly in the discussion of modernism in general; a disgust
with uniformity and a desire for diversity as an antidote.
Churchill is contrasted strongly with all of this:

> Churchill on the other hand emphasizes the moral
> heroism of empire, which brings nothing less than
> salvation to men who have never known the bless-
> ing of modernity. To bestow upon the primitive and
> ignorant the products of civilized intelligence is the
> richest gift one people can give another... British
> intelligence and British character equip the impe-
> rial soldiery to conquer peoples lacking those qual-
> ities, and to do so for their own good. Once the
> natives are vanquished in war, they are vouchsafed
> the healing benefits of peace.[4]

Churchill represents the belief, common at the time, in in-
evitable progress. People believed that progress was hard-wired
into nature, human nature, and history. The Bloombury group
represents the collapse into subjectivity that we have seen repeatedly, and is a hallmark of modernism.

In addition to the inversion of the mind and body, or nature and culture, we have also seen during the twentieth century
an inversion of the nineteenth century's secular idea of progress.
During the earlier time, progress was defined as movement from
primitive tribal social organization, as among Africans at the
time, to complex Western civilization with its moral religion,
elaborate legal system and abstract scientific knowledge. Hegel,
for instance, saw slavery as a progressive institution for Africans

---

[3]Ibid., 51.
[4]Ibid., 51-52.

because they were being acculturated into a more advanced civilization. We saw this with Churchill.

An example of this imagined hierarchy of "race" is shown in the film *Guess Who's Coming to Dinner* (1967). A Black woman objects to a marriage between a Black man and White woman because, as she says, "I don't want to see a member of my race getting above himself." Similarly, during the 1950s in the United States, African Americans embraced Western values. But starting during the 1960s, Blacks started to dress in African clothing and to adopt African names. This was seen as progressive-the eruption of the primitive into the landscape of the civilized or cultured. So movement from low to high was maintained from the old scheme, it was just the moral worth of the agents that changed.

So here we are, chained at the rock bottom of the cave and talking to the shadows. In act two of Wagner's music drama *Tristan and Isolde*, the titular couple sings for about 30 minutes about how unreal and fake day or light is, while darkness is the preferred condition or real. Darkness symbolizes desire, which for Wagner and many today was more real than lucidity or mind. Tristan sings in act 3, "The torch is extinguished! To her! To her!" And Isolde sings, "Unconscious, highest bliss!"

To show the power of hierarchy, both the nineteenth and twentieth century's concepts of "race" are structured by a Neoplatonic conception of hierarchy. Blackburn noted about Plotinus, a Neoplatonic philosopher, that:

> It is in contemplation of the higher, creative principle that the lower receives its form or impress. But it is also as reflections of the one cosmic Soul that individual souls exist, and their aim must be to direct their contemplation back up the hierarchy, eventually to obtain light and vitality by contemplative absorption of the One.[5]

---

[5] Simon Blackburn, *Oxford Dictionary of Philosophy* (New York: Oxford University, 2008), 280.

Another example of the elevation of nature is that, during the '60s, primitive art became elevated to fine art. Tribal art is irregular or assaulting, and so inspires reverence and modesty, like modern art. Nowadays Westerners pay homage to tribal and modern art wherein their sense of the regular is destroyed. Recall how Picasso used distorted tribal art to attack the Classical tradition and to remake art in its sexualized and redeemed version.

We see a similar fate for the human figure in art. Traditionally, it was considered the highest form of art, but today among academic modernism, it is stigmatized as commercial or low. This explains why in modern art the figure is usually presented as flattened and distorted or purified as in Byzantine art. One artist described a situation where he presented a drawing of a human hand to an instructor, and was criticized for it. He had succumbed to the temptation of beauty. Another student presented a drawing of an ape hand, and this the instructor praised. The bestial and the irregular is the ideal today and offers a vision of purgation or salvation from Western culture in the same way that looking at a picture of an angel was once purging or morally uplifting.

The modernist inversion is also reflected in in music. Modern music was ushered in 1907 with Schoenberg' *Pelleas und Melisande*. His 12-tone system attacked the beauty of traditional music and replaced it with noise whose only real value was redemption through subverting the dominant paradigm, as there was redemption through subverting the body. Schoenberg described his system as the "liberation of dissonance." This is consistent with the other forms of liberation that were occurring at this time.

Stravinsky's 1913 *Rite of Spring*, a ballet featuring a fertility rite and human sacrifice, also shows the inversion. The music's jagged dissonance and driving rhythms shocked most people and, according to the composer, caused a riot at the Paris premier.

The parallel with modern dance is clear as both represented the liberation of noise. Aaron Copland wrote his *Fanfare for the Common Man* and *An Outdoor Overture*. One music historian said that around 1900 "The young composers saw in Debussy a new Moses who could lead them from the bondage of traditional tonality and to the promised land of new music."[6] Notice the use of the well known religious narrative, also used by Martin Luther King, and the word *bondage* as in *confining*, a term we have seen regularly. The music of both Debussy and Stravinsky exemplify the collapse into subjectivity.

During the eighteenth century, musical forms were commonly derived from stylized dance forms, opera or rationalist sources, but starting in the early nineteenth century, literary and even the elements of nature start to inspire music. Mahler's Ninth Symphony was inspired by the composer's heart condition. As described earlier, Mahler the child wanted to be a martyr when he grew up. It seems that when he actually had to face death, his bravery faltered. Few would describe his Ninth Symphony as rousing and heroic. It is more an exercise in self-pity, another recurring theme of modernism.

As we have seen, nature was viewed as vulgar by the elite during the eighteenth century, and it would have been seen as inappropriate for music to be "polluted" by base and imperfect nature. When in college, I once played during a recital a nice piece of music on guitar. I then repeated the piece but exactly one fret up on the instrument creating a terrible noise. I loved this, and the audience applauded. When Brahms heard the premier of Mahler's first symphony, he asked, "Is this the future of music?" Joachim, the violinist who helped Brahms write his concerto for the instrument, said that the Sibelius concerto was "hideous and boring."

The fragmentation of form is also evident in popular or folk dance. In the eighteenth century, people danced in social forms

---

[6]Robert Greenberg, *How to Listen to and Understand Great Music*, 3rd edition, DVD lecture series (Chantilly VA: The Teaching Company, 2006).

resembling square dance or contra dance. Within a decade of the French revolution, the waltz roared into fashion, which critics described as "hugging set to music." Couples-based dancing remained the norm until the 1960s, when social dance fragmented completely and people started dancing individually or at some distance, with anyone who happened to be available. It is "hands off" today as no one wants to be oppressed by anyone else. In a film from the 1960s, a character says, "This is the twentieth century; no one possesses anyone else."

We see a similar fragmentation in the area of the family. In 1800, the average American family had 8 children. That figure steadily declined throughout the nineteenth century until it reached 2 children by 1940. There was a brief increase immediately after World War II, but by the 1960s it was down to 2 children again. With an emphasis on individual self-realization during the last two centuries, we see people less committed to a strong and demanding family life. It was once part of people's civic obligation to have large families, and the Biblical injunction was to be fruitful and multiply. Today, children are often seen as a nuisance.

Again, we see the recurring motif of claustrophobia, as in earlier discussion of Tolstoy and *Anna Karenina*. Commenting on the low fertility of upper-class people in the 1920s, Stoddard noted that, by promoting a strong eugenics movement, "People will think less about 'rights' and more about duties."[7]

Parents and for that matter children and teens think that youth rebellion or the bottom-up movement is morally justified. This reasoning, as we have seen, is common in popular and academic culture. Rebellious youth is a popular idea and image in the West today, and the subject of many films. No wonder people are resistant to parenthood.

We have seen a consistent picture of the nature of modernism in disparate areas of life, like the visual arts, ballet,

---

[7]Lothrop Stoddard, *The Revolt Against Civilization* (New York: Charles Scribner's Sons, 1923), 255.

popular film, music and political and social philosophy. As Chateaubriand said, "Without taste, genius is but sublime folly." This describes much of the non-scientific intellectual and cultural production of the last 150 years.

Predictably, folly is the today's ideal. In one pop song the woman sings, "Do you have street smarts, or are you just an intellect?" A professor in the book *The Dumbest Generation* noted that there is a strong trend of anti-intellectualism among the young today.[8] On the side of a building in Rome was a large banner that read, "I'm with stupid....be stupid." A 30 year old female attorney who was raised and educated in California said that it's fashionable to be a fool today.

To show how much attitudes and values have changed, Blacks in Hollywood film during the 1930s were often portrayed as lazy and stupid, and this was considered funny. But only for Blacks, not Whites. Nowadays, being lazy and stupid seem to be ideals for White Americans as well. Modernists do not want the mind and its regularities pressing down on anyone's freedom today. A Danish writer published a novel about a woman who had a sexual affair with a gorilla. This epitomizes the extent of the modernist aesthetic inversion. The West has gone from Homer's *Iliad* to a woman having sex with a gorilla.

According to Vasari, Michelangelo's Medici tomb would suffice to re-invent the art of sculpture:

> On one tomb he placed Night and Day, and on the other Dawn and Dusk; these statues are carved with the most beautifully formed poses and skillfully executed muscles and would be sufficient, if the art of sculpture were lost, to return it to its original splendor.[9]

[8]Mark Bauerlein, *The Dumbest Generation: How the Digital Age Stupefies Young Americans and Jeopardizes our Future* (New York: Penguin, 2008).

[9]Giorgio Vasari, Julia Bondanella and Peter Bondanella, trans., *Lives of*

When Vasari saw Michelangelo's sculpture the *Rondanini Pieta*, which is closer to a tree stump than to anything anyone could call beautiful, he knew art was fragile and that it could die fast. This is an obvious lesson from the history of the dark ages. Regarding the piety of modern art, what Vasari says about excessive moral zeal in art is informative:

> But I would not wish anyone to be mistaken and to construe that clumsy and inept works are pious, while beautiful and well-done ones are corrupt, as some people do when they see figures either of women or young boys that are a bit more pleasing, beautiful, and ornate than usual and who immediately seize upon them and judge them as lustful, without realizing that they are very much in the wrong to condemn the good judgment of the painter, who holds that the beauty of the saints, both male and female, who are celestial beings, surpasses that of mortal beings just as heavenly beauty surpasses our earthly beauty and our mortal works. But worse than this, they reveal their own infected and corrupted souls when they dig out evil and impure desires from these works, for if they were truly lovers of virtue, as they wish to prove by their foolish zeal, they would discern the painter's yearning for Heaven and attempt to make himself acceptable to the Creator of all things, from Whose most perfect and beautiful nature all perfection and beauty are born.[10]

As the beautiful was once praised because of its elevation from raw nature, modernists now praise the ugly and irregular because of the elevation of raw nature.

---

the Artists (New York: Oxford University, 2008.), 455-56.
[10]Ibid., 175.

Michelangelo himself was motivated by religion to attack art. In his *Rondanini Pieta* he portrays the Madonna and Christ in a manner that looks more like a Brancusi bird or, as stated, a tree stump than as an example of celestial beauty. That this is an attack is shown by an important element in the sculpture. Next to the figure group is a beautifully described male arm. It is fairly muscular and very realistic or beautiful, like his more famous works. Michelangelo juxtaposed an element of beauty next to something that looks essentially medieval and primitive. Nevertheless, the prominence of the figure group shows where his sympathies lie. Beauty is marginalized, and this it is clearly symbolic of his past sins or his early preoccupation with the beautiful body.

We see this logic in another of his works. In the painting the *Doni Tondo*, the Holy Family is in the foreground of the painting, while some nudes, who represent pagan antiquity, are in the far background. As the nudes represent past sins, the arm in the *Rondanini* represents the past sins of Michelangelo, or his preoccupation with the beauties of the body. So even in the short time span of the life of one man, art was able to meet a quick end, at least for Michelangelo; and it is no small thing that it was done by the hand of the man who did the most to show us the perfect body, as in the David.

As should be clear by now a new religion has formed in the West. What makes it different from other religions is that we can see its birth, for its birth is well documented, unlike the other religions whose origins are lost in the mists of time. It may be tempting to place the beginning of the religion of the individual at the French Revolution, but this is not in the historical record. None of the leaders of the revolution said that they were transforming man into God; but by the time of Victor Hugo, this is what people thought was going on in their lives, and thus projected it backwards onto the revolution. We saw this in the quote earlier from *Les Miserables* when the revolutionary said that the revolution was a consecration of man. Another character said that the revolutionaries were "giants" (p. 1154) or in other words were super-human. In the opera *Andrea Chenier* a character who participated in the revolution describes himself: "Pure, innocent and mighty, I thought myself a giant!" Purity! Will we ever escape it! And another character said that the revolution was to "Transform all men in God's own image!" (act three). Many Frenchmen today consider the revolutionaries as heroes. One French woman said a few years ago that, "We had to fight for everything we have." Similar speculation on the origins of religion is visible in antiquity.

Euhemerus was a Greek writer during the Hellenistic period who wrote a travel novel that some have interpreted as having a theory of the origins of religion. A group of sailors in the uncharted Indian Ocean comes across an island. They land and discover a column on which the deeds of Uranus, Cronus and Zeus are recorded. This gives the novel its title, *Sacred Scripture*. The column describes how Uranus, Cronus and Zeus had been great kings, and had received worship as Gods from a grateful people.

The novel is typically interpreted as a justification for Hellenistic ruler cult, or as a secular explanation for the origins of religion. The parallels with modernism are clear. First you have the heroes of the revolution, who represent the ascendency or rule of the individual. Then you have later writers like Hugo and the librettist of *Andrea Chenier* who turn them, and the individual into Gods. Recall here the characters in *Les Miserables* who believed that the men who fought in the revolution were "giants" and that the revolution was the "consecration of humanity." All of this was then projected backwards onto the revolution during the nineteenth century, and we saw this same process in *Sacred Scriptures* with the deification of the early kings. As the early kings ascended to Godhead, so has the individual today. To put it another way, Hugo and others were writing foundation myths in the same way that modern feminist scholars today rewrite history to create for women some large role, again with no foundation in the record, a foundation myth for modern feminism. This rewriting of history is a central activity for many academics or mythographers.

Why is this so easy for people? It reflects the mind on automatic. Recall the connection between self and mind and the group, and that the sense of agency could move back and forth. Similarly, if God could exist "out there" up in the clouds, then agency could be moved into the individual body, resulting in its deification.

Chapter 5

PC: The Greatest Show on Earth

Let me put it this way: the five films nominated for Best Picture for 1975 were *One Flew Over the Cuckoo's Nest, Barry Lyndon, Dog Day Afternoon, Jaws,* and *Nashville.* Well, not the greatest ever made...[but] it was a pretty good year. I won't take the space to list the ten films the Academy scrounged together for Best picture this last year, because so few of them stand company with what 1975 had to offer.

— David Thomas

The New Biographical Dictionary of Film, 2010

As we have seen, film provides many examples of our new debased morals. This chapter focuses on several films and how they illustrate the creation and work of the social body, its encroaching evil, and how we rebel against it. It works chronologically, starting with older films and working its way later in time.

In the silent film *The Eagle* (1925) Rudolph Valentino plays a Russian Robin Hood named Vladimir Dubrovsky. At the be-

ginning, Dubrovsky is in the special guard of the Czarina. She
asks to see him in private, and as part of a sexual advance,
she kisses him. This he finds revolting, leaves the palace and
goes AWOL. Out of pique, she issues a warrant for his arrest.
Dubrovsky then receives a letter from his father that describes
how an evil landlord has confiscated his father's estate, leaving him penniless. The father asks Dubrovsky to try to obtain
assistance from the Czarina. This of course is impossible because Dubrovsky just walked out on her. This conflict is the last
straw for Dubrovsky, and he dons a black mask and declares
war against the landlord and his representatives who robbed his
father, all the while trying to avoid arrest from the Russian Government. As the rebel, he becomes known as the "Black Eagle"
and he forms a band of loyal followers who help him to harass
the landlord and his servants. At one point, Dubrovsky robs a
man who works for the landlord. So we see that the system
or the social body is corrupt and that the only thing a man of
virtue can do is fight against it. There is a music group today
called "Thievery Corporation." Rebellion is romanticized in the
film, as is common today, and as people in earlier times used
to romanticize rebellion against the body and its corruption. Of
course, social body rebellion derives from the older belief, as
we saw how modernism has simply recast the battle between
good and evil. Instead of the high against the low, it is now the
low against the high.

There is a historical example of people opposing the upper classes because of sexual transgression. One factor that inflamed the Parisian masses during the French revolution was
that Maria-Antoinette crossed the border between virgin and
whore. The French Kings had traditionally had their wives appear very plain, and the wives' role was as devoted mother and
upholder of religion. In addition, the king was allowed to have
a mistress that he could doll up, or who played the whore. This
maintained the Madonna/whore dichotomy. Louis XVI made
the mistake of dolling up his wife, and this mixing up of the traditional roles inflamed the moral senses of the Parisian people.

This was not the only cause of the Revolution, of course, but it was factor, as we saw with Dubrovsky and his reaction to the Czarina.

In another Valentino silent film that takes place in Algeria, *The Sheik* (1921), an Englishman says to an English woman, "I love you, let's get married." The woman responds, "Marriage is captivity, the end of independence." Recall here the example from *Sex and the City* when Carry Bradshaw is trying on a wedding dress, falls to the floor and yells, "I'm suffocating, I'm suffocating!" and quickly removes the dress. The second chapter presented many examples of society or the social body as confining or claustrophobic. The traditional cry "Babylon!" or captivity to sin became "Society!" the new sin or captivating source of corruption to rebel against. Later on in the film the English woman is kidnapped by "the sheik" played by Valentino. At first, she resists him, but after they get to know each other, and he performs several heroic deeds, she falls in love with him. At the end of the film, they unite in love, and things point in the direction of marriage.

In the sequel, *The Son of the Sheik* (1925), Valentino plays both the original sheik, now age 50, and his own son. Most of the film is about the tribulations that the son undergoes over a woman, but toward the end of the film the father is holding his English wife in his arms, and she says wistfully, "Remember when you were young, and you grabbed what you wanted." She is alluding to her own kidnapping at his hands when they were young. It is clear that, although she resisted her kidnapping at the time, at some level she liked it. (Bride abduction is still practiced in some Muslim countries.) Her acquiescence contrasts with the opening scene of the first film where she rejects the honest advances of the civilized Englishman. This is "captivity" but her literal abduction by a wild Arab is exciting. By the end of the second film, it becomes clear that she does not mind captivity, only a certain form of it. She does not want to be the wife of an uptight Englishman and chained to some dreary house in England. She wants to be in captivity to a wild

man with a sword and gun strapped to his side and who lives
in a tent in the middle of the desert and commands a horde of
men. This is a more physical captivity, with greater danger, and
less of a social captivity or confinement to the social body. We
have seen the theme of the body repeatedly in modernism. If
we were to ask Tolstoy's opinion, we would know who the real
man is-who is the one to get excited about. In the context of
our regular cultural values, we know which man represents the
irregular and which is the hero.

Another film about heroes is the World War One drama *All
Quiet on the Western Front* (1930). It starts with a group of
young German men in a school room being lectured to by a
older man who goes into detail about the virtues of heroism, and
that there is nothing sweeter than to die for one's country. The
young men decide to volunteer for the army but soon learn that
the training is hard work. Twice while marching they must fall
into the mud. Even before they have seen any action they get fed
up with the training, and one of the men calls the drill sergeant
a "filthy ape." This use of low imagery to a high context should
sound familiar. As police today are pigs, so drill sergeants are
apes.

The men decide to take revenge on the drill sergeant. At
night when he is out by himself, they tie him up, put a sack over
his head and dump him in some mud. He suffers at the hands of
his own sins, a common theme in Christian and Greco-Roman
morality as we will see.

In one of the first scenes at the front, a bunker frequently
leaks dirt on their heads because of bomb explosions and, most
horribly, at one point a swarm of rats invades the bunker. The
men groan and complain throughout the scene. The first 45 minutes of the movie, before any military action, comprises scenes
like this of horrible suffering. Of course, the under-current of
the film has a tone of rebellion, and this often breaks out, even
during eating scenes.

At one point, the film explicitly romanticizes insubordi-
nation. An officer comes into the bunker and demands to be

saluted. The men ignore him. One pulls down his pants and aims his buttocks in the officer's direction. This is his salute.

One of the most ridiculous scenes in the film is when a German soldier is in fox hole and a French soldier drops inside of it. The German takes out a knife and stabs him. Not sure that he's dead, the German starts to talk to him and eventually apologizes for the assault, and he even prays and apologizes to God for the assault.

During a lull in the action, the soldiers bathe in a river and some French girls come walking by on the opposite bank. The men start to yell in a flirtatious way and try to make dates. Another soldier who is on guard sees this and warns the men that they cannot cross the river. The men show the girls that they have food, and this gets the girls' attention, and who then agree to meet them later. That evening, there is a scene in a house with the men and girls eating and drinking, and clearly there is hanky-panky. The message is clear: make love not war. This is depicted as real, as opposed to the fighting which is the false consciousness of zealous nationalism or social anger or hate, one the deadly sins for modernism.

After over an hour and half of the horrors of war, the main character, Paul, finally starts to make explicitly anti-war statements. While on leave he visits the classroom of the teacher who convinced him and the others to join. The teacher encourages Paul to praise war, but Paul simply describes how horrible it is, and says, "When it comes to dying for your country, it is better to not die at all." The other students look at him with disapproval and call him a coward. Then he says what may be the thesis of the film, "Death is stronger than duty to one's country." As the suffering and death of Jesus were absolute horrors, and could trump duty to ones country and leaders, we see this logic working here, with the individual being Jesus of course.

As people used to plead on behalf of Jesus, now they plead on behalf of themselves. As it was horrible that Jesus died for our sins, now it is horrible that people die at the hands of the social body, or social hubris, one of the deadly sins. This is the

source of the evasiveness, complaining and cowardice throughout the film. As people strained to avoid the suffering of Jesus,
now they desperately want to avoid their own suffering, and do
not want to be oppressed. This is why people dance almost
alone today. Traditionally, duty to one's country was seen as
part of duty to God; as in "God and Country." The traditional
hierarchy was such that national leaders and their orders were
up there with God. Nationalism and religion were entangled
for most people in the nineteenth and early twentieth centuries.
With the rise of natural rights and popular sovereignty, we have
seen religion bent to different purposes as is clearly illustrated
by the film.

The film *From Here to Eternity* (1953), which takes place in
Hawaii in the days before the Pearl Harbor attack, is not anti-
war, which would have been nearly impossible in the years after the success of American forces in World War Two, but it is
clearly anti-military. The impression one gets from the film is
that the military embodies abuse of power. In the film, the Army
is a surrogate for the social body. The film portrays the military
hierarchy as corrupt to the point that it kills its own people. The
hero of the film, Robert Prewitt played by Montgomery Clift,
refuses to box for his regiment's team. The commanding officer
tries to convince him to fight but Prewitt refuses. The officer
and his underlings make life difficult for Prewitt as incentive to
get him to fight. At one point, Prewitt is scrubbing the floor,
and a low-ranking officer kicks over two buckets of dirty water,
and then yells at Prewitt, "Clean it up!" Prewitt becomes angry,
and refuses. The commanding officer orders Prewitt to apolo-
gize to the officer who kicked the buckets, but Prewitt says that
it ought to be he that is apologized to. This is part of the strategy of the commanding officer to force Prewitt to box. Later, in
his office, the commanding officer is arranging special punishment for Prewitt for disobeying orders, and says, "Men like him
can't be treated decently, but must be treated like an animal."
Of course, we know here who is abusing power, and is thus an
"animal."

While on leave, Prewitt's character meets Lorene Burke, played by Donna Reed. They fall in love, but Burke resists marrying someone of such low status. She says that she wants to earn money from her job, buy a proper house, join a proper golf club, meet and marry a proper man of status, and have proper children. Her reason for this is that "When you're proper, you're safe." The significance of this becomes clear near the end of the film.

Frank Sinatra plays Angelo Maggio, a character who likes to drink. At one point, Maggio gets into a bar fight with Fatso, a guard at the local stockade. Eventually Maggio goes AWOL and is sentenced to 6 months in the stockade, where Fatso beats him mercilessly whenever they are alone. The situation is enough to make you sympathize with the storming of the Bastille. Eventually, Maggio breaks out of the stockade but is injured in the process. He finds Prewitt and as he dies in Prewitt's arms, he tells of the abuse he suffered and how he spat in Fatso's face every time he was beaten. He describes how he escaped and perishes. He is portrayed as a victim of the military's cruel abuse of power. As the body made Jesus suffer, now the social body or social hubris, makes us suffer. The scene with the dead Maggio draped in Prewitt's arms resembles a modernist Pieta.

Prewitt then fights Fatso and kills him, but is injured in the process. While he is recuperating in Burke's house, the Japanese attack Pearl Harbor. Though injured, Prewitt decides to go back to the Army to help fight the Japanese. As he is leaving Burke's house, she becomes hysterical with fear for Prewitt's life. She describes that he is injured and that going into battle will open the wound; then she says that if he goes back the Army will put him in the stockade for Fatso's murder. She offers to marry him. With this offer, we see that she has given up her shallow class aspirations and decided to be real. She then says, "The Army treated you like dirt" and "they killed your friend." At this point, it is clear that the abuse was not the responsibility of a few bad people but the entire institution of the Army. As the Virgin Mary grief-stricken over the death of Jesus, now Burke is hysterical with grief at the impending death of Prewitt at the hands of the social body. In the last scene, Prewitt is gunned down by a US soldier for not obeying an order to halt. In the end, he is killed, not by the Japanese, but by his own military. This vindicates Burke's hysterical concerns. As the body was once sure death, so now is the social body.

The modern Christian morality we saw in *All Quite on the Western Front* and *From Here to Eternity* generates today the same paranoid fantasy iconography as it did with old master paintings of hell. Today, as during the Renaissance, there is iconography representing the mortality that people will suffer if they follow their deep desires, believe in their social system and military, and satisfy its needs, succumbing to its desires.

The film *The Terminator* (1984) partly takes place in a future when the West's military defense systems have taken over and turned against people. The military computers kill everyone foolish enough to have believed in them and did not disarm-who did not repress their social body's desires. To make people suffer for their sins, the defense systems inflict mortality on people instead of protecting them and the interests of civilization.

As the glutton in Bosch's *The Garden of Earthly Delights* is devoured by a huge stomach on legs, the social body's military systems set out to exterminate humanity for having created them to dominate and kill them for having succumbed to their social body. The West suffers at the hands of the sins themselves.

The film presents images of hell on earth to foreshadow the future damnation. In the *Book of Revelation*, the sins of our bodies cause the destruction of the Earth. So today the sins of the social body cause the destruction of the Earth. Mortality and its symbols are in full view for people as a warning of what they will receive for having succumbed.

In Dante's *Inferno*, the gluttonous live on heaps of garbage under driving storms of cold rain, while flatterers are immersed in pools of sewage, and the sexually perverse walk burning stretches of sand in an environment as sterile as their attempts at love.

In *The Terminator*, the social body's urges dominate. People live in folly, so the wages of sin is total annihilation by the sin of social anger itself. People are killed and tortured by their earthly pleasures.

In response to the attack by the social body, exhausted, demoralized humans go underground to fight a losing guerrilla war, a war against the force of mortality that ceaselessly descends. The desolate battleground where people meet their mortality is strewn with the bones and skulls of the millions who have died at the hands of their own defense system, their sins.

In the arena where humans face death, their descent, symbols of their mortality are in view as warning. Closely framed images show tanks rolling over skulls and incinerating or burning people with lasers. People burn for their sins. People die for having sinned and believed in society's project of civilization and its defense, for living for this life. Those who live suffer endless pain inflicted by their own sins. The battle scenes do not depict battles like those in World War II films, but are stylized and symbolic of gloom and doom. Humans live underground, while the machines or the military control the surface of the earth. What is righteous is revolt from below, as we saw earlier. Only this movement is legitimate; the movement up of good against evil.

If people had repressed their social body and disarmed, they would have had life, true immortality in the future. They would have gone to heaven instead of hell. As Christians once needed to fight the body's desire to sin, everyone now must fight the social body's desire for a military, now and in the future-the military body, quite literally, in this case. We see this sentiment in embryonic form in *From Here to Eternity*. This battle against the military is a graphic, literal example of the battle that people must wage if eternal life is to be had.

But there is a light: People can be saved from their sins through Jesus.

In the film, a robot-agent of the social body goes back in time to the present pre-apocalyptic era to kill Sarah Connor, a woman who will give birth to a boy who will be a super-leader of the humans during their future battle against the social body. To protect her and their future leader, the humans send Kyle Reese back in time to subvert the assassin. Appearing out of nowhere, he desperately searches for the woman, who is oblivious of the folly of her social body, unaware that she is going to be devoured by the social body in its future attempts to kill her, and ignorant of her sacred mission to give birth to the savior.

She is busy having a good time. Connor is just a regular woman, not "conscious" of her mission to give birth to the boy who will lead the successful battles against the social body in the future, who will save people from their sins and give them the strength to fight their sins. She is not conscious of the folly of her social body.

When Reese and Connor finally meet, he tells her of the sins of the social body and announces to her that she is to give birth to a son who will be the leader, the savior in the future, the man who will save people from their sin. She thinks that Reese is crazy as he seeks to raise her consciousness of her mission. After repeated attacks from the robot, she becomes convinced that the man came to protect and enlighten her. Together, they finally destroy the robot, the social body. The authority of the human body-the will to resist the temptations of the social body-temporarily triumphs.

The hero Reese dies in the process of saving the woman from herself, from her lack of consciousness, for her future and the future of mankind. He dies for our sins, but her consciousness of the sins of the social body has been heightened. In the final scene, the woman moves to a humble, alternative desert country, where people speak Spanish, to escape the social body and raise her son, the savior. She is pregnant as she drives a Jeep Renegade. She is a warrior or rebel against society. We see the simple anti-war message of *All Quite on the Western Front* raised in intensity to a fantasyland narrative and iconography of anti-militarism.

In the Bible, an angel tells Mary that she is to give birth to a Child who is going to be the Savior of the world. She is startled, protesting that she is of humble birth. Eventually, she is persuaded of her mission. In *The Terminator*, the man who appears and announces that she is to give birth has sex with her, and thus sires the savior. This is an echo or humanization of the original Biblical annunciation scene where the Holy Spirit enters the Virgin with prompting from the angel.

In the Bible, after giving birth, Mary hides herself and the child because the state (Herod) has given orders to destroy all baby boys born on the same day as Jesus: In *The Terminator*, the agent of the social body kills all women with the same name as Connor in an attempt to stop the Savior. "How early did persecution commence against Christ and his Kingdom!" as someone said during the nineteenth century.

Each woman, Mary and Connor, gives birth to a boy who will save Christendom from their sins, the sins of either their human or social body. *The Terminator* is a modern polyptych: *The Slaughter of the Innocents, The Last Judgment, The Annunciation,* and *The Flight into Egypt.* Until this century, people were largely illiterate, and Christianity and its narratives were people's basic education.

The sequel to *The Terminator* was appropriately titled *JudgmentDay.* It tells how figures reflecting Mary, Jesus, and Joseph try to destroy the social body before "judgment day," as they refer to it in the film-that is, the day the social body takes over and inflicts hell on earth.

Some interesting differences in this film from its antecedent are that the Connor, Mary figure, has choices in her life (she has triumphed over her social body and is a hero) and a handsome, clean-cut policeman represents the stalking, evil social body. The Joseph figure (a re-programmed beneficent terminator robot) looks like a motorcycle gang member. The movie implies that people should not succumb to their social body and believe that evil looks evil and good looks good. After all, modernists claim that White men and the police are evil. Motorcycle gang members are beautiful, while the police are pigs, the evil agents of the social body. Sarah Connor has a more active role in this film, taking on much of the fighting. Her back-story says that in the past she tried to blow up a computer factory. In the first film, both of the main characters were blonds, but their son in the second film appears to be part Asian.[1] We see a blow for diversity, regardless of the facts, as with the emotional Scandinavian and restrained Italian in *Titanic*. There are almost no Blacks in the first film, not even as extras, whereas in the second film there are many, including one who is important to the plot. When Connor, the Mary figure, talks to the man responsible for creating the technology that will try to destroy mankind in the future, she says, "it is men like you who destroy life, while women create life." The film depicts men as the evil social body, while women are good, representing the body.

At the film's climax, Connor and the good terminator robot destroy with axes the computer lab that will create the machines that will try to exterminate mankind. This resembles the tactics used by Carrie Nation, a leader of the early temperance movement. Around 1900, she would go into bars and destroy them with an axe. She raised money for the movement by selling miniature axes and by the publicity that resulted from her prison time. Both women are heroes against evil: for Carrie Nation the evils of the body, for Sarah Connor the evils of the social body. In the film, Sarah and the good terminator fight desperately for their lives, and she is often almost hysterical with fear. Reflecting Christianity, the film's Jesus, Mary, and Joseph figures, by their example, inspire others in their battles against sin. This reflects that today modernists experience the military as an evil or fearful imposition.

In the earlier film *The Santa Fe Trail* (1940), an officer tells a group of junior officers: "We here at Fort Leavenworth are the only military installation between here and Santa Fe, and we

---

[1]Editor's note: The child John Connor is played by Edward Furlong, whose mother is Mexican and father is Russian.

are proud of that responsibility." Today, people would complain about being understaffed, victimized, and oppressed, and would conclude that they deserve danger pay.

In the film, the fort and the men who occupy it are inseparable: "We here...are the only military installation." The men are the military installation. The fort is an extension of its occupants and does not oppress them or bear down on top of them as in modern imagery. It does not have an adversarial relationship as in *From Here to Eternity* and *Terminator*.

Today, when the military wants to inspire people, it mentions that if they do not fight, they will be killed by the enemy- or worse, they will not receive their college tuition scholarship. The old perspective is that the interests of superior civilization and its defense are the interests of all, even non-Westerners because of the reigning idea of progress.

The film *Saving Private Ryan* (1998) is anti-war in an oblique fashion. It takes place during the Normandy invasion of World War II, so it would be hard to portray the American cause as evil, but the film's plot argues that there are more important things, as in *All Quite on the Western Front*. The opening scene shows the landing, and instead of the soldiers heroically running off the landing ships and attacking the Germans, the soldiers vomit and are cut to pieces by German machine gun and artillery fire. Three or four scenes show limbs blown off and men lying in the water with their guts hanging out. John Miller, a captain played by Tom Hanks, has a hand that shakes throughout the film. The issue here is emphasis. Obviously there were many fatalities during the landing, but the allies were successful. The impression you get from the scene is that it was a failed cause. The scene would have been perfect for *All Quite on the Western Front*: war is nothing more than horror and futile loss of life.

The surviving men huddle behind a hill of sand and eventually penetrate the German line of defense. Once they have made a beachhead, the film cuts to a meeting of General Marshal and his staff. A Mrs. Ryan has lost three of her sons in the fighting, while the fate of her fourth and last is unknown. Marshal concludes that Private Ryan must be pulled out of the fighting at almost any cost. A special unit is formed from the Normandy force to save Private Ryan and is commanded by Captain Miller. Nothing at the beginning or end of the film says that it was based on true story, so we can take it as the product of the same imagination that produced *All Quite on the Western Front*. The plot implies that the entire war effort was put on hold for one person. For over an hour, the unit roams around the villages of Normandy looking for Ryan, occasionally fighting German troops.

Now one need not rely on the plot nor the action to see the film's preference of the individual over the collective war effort. Statements are to this effect. For instance, at one point Miller says, "I am willing to lay down my life and those of my men to ease the suffering of Ryan's mother." At the end of the film he does indeed die with most of his men, but Ryan, whom they find, survives. At the film's mid-point, Captain Miller tells a soldier that one rational for a war action is that it can save more lives than it costs: "This is how you rationalize the choice between the mission and the man." The soldier responds, "But this time the mission is the man." As Jesus was the all-consuming mission now the individual is. Recall here John Stuart Mill's belief that the individual is above the state and is to be served by the state. It would be hard to find a clearer example of this philosophy than this film.

A soldier in the film makes an even more emphatic statement when he says, "Saving Private Ryan was the one decent thing we were able to pull off from this God awful shitty mess. We do that then we all earn the right to go home." Now I think it is fairly obvious that defeating the Germans was more important and more decent, but not according to modernist philosophy. We could have lost Private Ryan, and if we had defeated the Germans, the war would still have been a success though apparently it would have been indecent. Decency, in the eyes of some today, lies not with survival of our institutions, the social body, but with the suffering individual-the Christ-type and model of decency. We know who is on top of the state today in their eyes.

At one point, to convince Ryan to quit the fighting and go home with the special unit, a man says to Ryan, "two men died to find you." Now this statement is amazing in light of the events at the end of the film. There is a large battle between an outnumbered special unit and a well armed and manned German unit. During the course of the fighting almost all of the Americans are killed except Ryan. So not just two, but over a dozen men are killed "saving Private Ryan." The film ends the way it began, with an implied heroic ethic. As people wanted to immolate themselves over Jesus, now it is over the all-powerful individual. This is what modernists want to fight for today, and this prompts major currents in political thought such as among the libertarians, and in lesser degrees among most people, and prompts the mania over civil rights on both the left and right. Hence, we have ACLU defending the right of Mexicans to invade the United States. It is the decent thing to do, at least from one maniacal perspective.

In the film *Tears Of The Sun* (2003), a departing U.S. military unit cannot bring itself to abandon a destitute and threatened African people, and so it returns to rescue them. Recall here that as Christians wanted to fight for God, now the protagonists want to fight for Blacks. In an episode of *Friends*, Phoebe, Ms New Age, throws herself in front of a dart gun aimed at a monkey. In another episode, she hysterically stops Joey from putting a dead Christmas tree into a wood chipper. The series makes clear that such actions by Phoebe express a form of devotion integral to her fanatical personality. In *Tears Of The Sun*, team leader Lieutenant A.K. Waters, played by Bruce Willis, gets misty when viewing a field of dead Africans. He decides to help the Africans and come to their rescue. His unit inadvertently saves a king by their military actions. Waters certainly is a faithful servant. A Black soldier tells Waters, "Those are my people" as moral justification for helping them, and Willis adds that his men should fight, "for our sins," as if for redemption. So much for the "modern" world.

What is significant about this film is that it is pro-military and pro-war. What matters is what the soldiers fight for. When the cause is Blacks, or fighting for redemption from the sins of the social body, then fighting and death are portrayed in a positive light. When fighting is presented as the expression of traditional European nationalism, or any other form of self-centeredness, then it is just a horror, as we saw in *All Quite on the Western Front* and *Terminator*.

Another important element of the film is that the military unit helps the African group against orders from superiors. In other words, they are themselves rebels, rebelling from below in order to help the low. At one point, Lt. Waters says, "It's the same mission," to morally justify his rebellious action by drawing a parallel with the official mission. Only the rebellion from below is righteous or morally justified. If, in a different context, the military unit had gone against orders and helped the conservative Contras fight against the Sandinistas of Nicaragua, it would have been viewed as horrible by Hollywood liberals. It would have been in the interest of the United States, but that is just a horror. When Waters is asked why he does it, he responds that he "does not have it figured out." This statement is worth pausing over. This is similar to the statement from Rose in *Titanic* on how the Picasso has truth but no logic, and, most importantly, that going off with Jack, "makes no sense, but that's why I trust it."

It is clear that modernists on both the left and right do not know what they are doing, and instead are on automatic emotion, reasoning, and action, like an animal. Science is nowhere to be seen in the modern world as it pertains to human nature, action, morals, and politics. The end of *Tears Of The Sun* has a quotation usually attributed to 18th-century philosopher Edmund Burke: "The only thing necessary for the triumph of evil is for good men to do nothing." We see that the battle against evil, or at least a new notion of evil, is the driving engine or heart of modernism and its moralizing films and politics.

A more sophisticated and fantastic development of the same metaphor of evil from the social body is the movie *Alien* (1979). A ship belonging to a private company is traveling through space when it receives radio signals from a nearby planet. As part of the crew's contract with the social body, they must search for the source of the transmission or forfeit their pay. Against their best instincts, they land on the planet. For "selling out" in this way, they are doomed. They have sold their souls to the Devil.

The crew enters a derelict ship on the planet's surface and finds pods containing large, crablike creatures. One creature leaps from a pod and latches onto the face of a crewman, inserting a tentacle down the victim's throat and into his chest and stomach. His mates bring him back to the ship, where they attempt to remove the creature. However, after a day of failed effort, the creature dies and falls off.

The victim becomes conscious and appears to be normal, joining the rest of the crew for dinner. Suddenly the man collapses in convulsions on the table, screaming in pain as a baby reptilian monster eats its way through his chest to emerge and slither away while the terrified crewmembers watch. The baby grows within hours to become a huge carnivorous monster that stalks the crew and devours them one by one.

In an attempt to gather helpful data from the computer to fight the monster, a female crewmember discovers that the company had planned to sacrifice the crew in order to bring the monster back to civilization. With the aid of a White male (robot) science officer, the company (the social body) brings evil into the world from the outside, with innocents falling victim.

They deposit evil into the body and back out again, creating evil in the world: monsters. The social body is evil, and succumbing to the social body creates evil in the world. If the crew had ignored the transmission, gone on strike, repressed the social body, then evil would have been frustrated. Westerners must be ascetic and deprive their social body to repress evil. The crew succumbed to the social body, sinned, and fell to Earth. Recall that in medieval art the dragon angrily consumes his victims. The dragon of the Vikings and then of the Christians has become the dragon of society.

In *Alien*, a powerful voice against going onto the planet is that of the Black male mechanic. He naturally resists the urges of the social body, but is ultimately victimized by it. To whom should the West listen? To evil White men or righteous and beautiful Black men? That is easy, "Black is beautiful." Black men are hip to the real agenda, the evil with which White men want to infest people's lives. Middle-class White men are evil, while lower-class men, like in Titanic, and especially Black men, are heroes.

Another important difference between the old and new process of evil is the kind of presence that evil has in the body. Two 19th-century creations, Frankenstein's monster and Dracula, derived from Christian tradition of witches, goblins, and ghosts, and so were inseparable from their evil. Evil permeated the very fiber of their bodies. In fact, evil was their bodies. Frankenstein's monster had the brain of a crazed murderer, and Dracula was compared to a wild animal.

The plot of the 1931 film version of *Dracula* is a good example of how people at the time thought about evil. Dracula has no reflection in a mirror and can take on the form of a bat or a wolf. He is dead and evil and so cannot stand the sight of either daylight or the cross. Dracula's evil is contagious. The people he bites become vampires themselves. This derives from the popular idea that emotion was contagious temptation. At one point Dracula tries to dominate a man, but the man resists, and Dracula compliments him in his strength to resist the power of Dracula. (Women uniformly succumb.) The same man eventually figures out what Dracula is doing and drives a stake through his heart to kill him. When Dracula is destroyed, the spell that he has over people is broken. With this in mind, consider that in 16th-century France, 50,000 so-called werewolves were executed. Suspects were men with hair between their eyebrows who kept to themselves. People took evil so seriously, that it generated collective fantasies or images and dictated church and government policy. Witch trials also come to mind here.

At the beginning of the *Dracula* film, the first person that the vampire bites says, with a possessed tone of voice and look on his face, that he will be loyal to Dracula, and that Dracula is his master. The person has become a slave to evil or sin. We saw how this idea was transformed in political theory during the eighteenth century by the idea that the lower classes were good and needed freedom from the enslaving evil of the upper classes. As the slogan in Dracula is "Freedom from evil or death," the political slogan starting during the eighteenth century, was "Freedom or Death."

As Dracula was depicted as subhuman or inferior, so is the upper class today. The phrase, "great blond beast," was used to refer to Germans during the Second World War. College student draft deferments were suspended during the Vietnam War, and Charles Murray in his recent book on education said that smart students are not superior, just lucky.[2]

Anti-elitism has become ever stronger during the past century, even among conservatives like the military and Charles Murray. Dr. Murray may be caving in to the hate mail he received for co-authoring *The Bell Curve*, which describes how intelligence determines social class or status. As we saw that it was evil for Whites to offend Blacks, now we see that it is taboo for smart Whites to get uppity with dumb Whites, or for the upper class to get uppity with the lower. Recall here that most wealthy people are democrats because they want to be politically fashionable or seen to have the proper morals and high status. Today, the high identify with the low, instead of the tradition whereby the lower classes tried to improve themselves by imitating the upper. We see this reversal in the deference relationship between White and Black Americans. Victor Hugo's class bashing universal love so strenuously argued for

---

[2]Charles Murray, *Real Education* (New York: Crown Forum, 2008).

in *Les Miserables* has triumphed. Who would want to impose misery on anyone? Of course to believe otherwise would be succumbing to the social body which is seen as evil, like the Nazis. Regarding the prospect of resurrecting eugenics policies, one writer said, "that went *down* [italics added] with the Nazis." Nowadays, the elite are the "great blond beast," subhuman or low, while everyone loving each other, regardless of characteristics, is "high," righteous or sublime in order to defeat the social body.

The film *Rabid* (1977) translates the tale of Dracula into the new Christian moral causality of social body determinism. The movie opens with a meeting of male plastic surgeons plotting to become the "McDonald's of plastic surgery." The head surgeon leaves the meeting and performs an experimental method of plastic surgery on a woman. The procedure is faulty-evil-and she goes into a deep coma. After waking, she has grown a small set of jaws in the area of the incision.

When she has a hunger for blood, she embraces her victim and the jaws come out. The people who are victimized, including the doctor, become rabid, but then die. She eventually escapes the hospital and proceeds to infect the entire city.

Again, the message is that the social body creates monsters, evil in the body and in people's lives. When the woman begins to understand what she does to people, she cries in protest, "But it's not my fault!" She is a victim of the urges of the evil social body. The social body causes evil to which people fall victim. "Society made me do it!" says the criminal.

Bram Stoker's Dracula was innately evil and therefore was logically created from the innately evil body. If today society creates human evil, then logically it should also create Dracula. As Jesus said that sinful actions are just the outward sign of what people are inside, the evil actions of the *Rabid* lady Dracula are just the inward sign of what she is outside.

For the new Christian monsters, evil has a quantifiable presence in the body. The innocent body can be opened up, and evil can be viewed and removed. What was once human folly is now a quantifiable mental disorder or mental victimization. "The Devil made me do it" has turned into "Society is in me and made me do it." Today, people must go to a psychologist—a modern priest—to purge the evil from their minds. In *Dracula* evil is contagious, and in *Rabid* we see that the social body is contagious. People's impulses come from out there, from social institutions like class, gender, and "race." As described earlier, with the redemption of sex and the body by the 1960s, the displacement of evil and agency was easy to make because of the connection between felt emotion and the emotions of the vocabulary of body images in the mind and those of our peers.

The dragon of society is seen as pure evil, as are the men who create it. Evil emanates from White men, makes people's lives imperfect, and permeates their bodies. White men are the source of people's mortality.

The causality of evil in *Alien* is identical to the model of moral causality in *Rabid*. In both films, the imperfect plotting social body puts evil into people, only to have it emerge from and create evil in the world. Not only is the causality identical in both films, but the physical process that creates evil is also identical: evil is placed within people, and then literally protrudes from the body.

As in the old Christian schema, the body is an important point of evil in these films. But how the body obtains that state has become complicated for mythmakers, creating a need for narrative to explain how the body comes to the condition of evil, how it is victimized by the social body. The body is innocent or beautiful, but the state, larger business institutions, and White males who are their active agents are evil. The new narrative of the victim is why modern films seem sophisticated compared to the traditional stereotyped portrayals of pure evil bodies.

The film *Ghost in the Machine* (1993) shows displacement of evil. A psychotic killer dies in a MRI machine, and his spirit goes into the machine. He then spends the rest of the film conducting a reign of terror against people through their machines; for instance, a man is burned to death by his microwave oven, and another is burned alive by a hand dryer. We see that people do not kill people, but machines do. The reasoning is similar to *Terminator*. It also generates the mania for gun control. The NRA combats this with the slogan that "Guns don't kill people; People kill people" but this obvious assertion goes against our intuitions today.

Similarly, the disaster film genre came into existence during the 1970s. Two well-known examples are *The Poseidon Adventure* (1972) and *The Towering Inferno* (1974). The technological structures in the films-a ship and a skyscraper-while appearing safe, turn out to be, respectively, a whirlpool and an oven that close in on people and become their tombs. The social body only spells doom so it is best to not be a dupe.

In *Alien*, the monster's main opponent is a woman. Modernists believe that women are on the cutting edge. At the end of the film, the woman triumphs against the monster of the social body. In both *Alien* and *Terminator* women play a decisive role in defeating the social body, just as they have this role in the popular imagination in combating the social body in politics.

Today women are more progressive than men. There is even a recent book by an irate White male entitled *In Fifty Years We'll All Be Chicks*. As men used to dominate women before the twentieth century because women were viewed as earthy and more emotional, today women dominate because they are more progressive or in tune due to their association with Earth and the emotions. Nowadays men are seen as subhuman or male chauvinist pigs like Dracula. At some level women fear men as they fear death or entrapment, instead of looking up to men as they did in the nineteenth century. As we have seen, this fear is a common theme in *Sex and the City*. Again, we see a reversal or inversion.

A film at the top of the inversion list is *Gran Torino* (2008). Clint Eastwood plays Walt Kowalski, an elderly Korean War veteran who initially hates non-Whites in general and in particular his Asian neighbors. A young man in the Asian family, named Thao, tries to steal Kowalski's Gran Torino car but

Kowalski stops him. In compensation, the Asian family makes Thao work for Kowalski. Kowalski and Thao become friends, and at one point Kowalski says that he has more in common with the Asian family than he does with his own "spoiled, rotten family". This shows a major transformation for Kowalski in his attitudes to non-Whites. Kowalski also says that he is proud to have Thao as a friend. At one point Kowalski starts to offer Thao advice on dating, and goes so far as to offer Thao the use of the Gran Torino for a date. In addition, he changes his will and leaves the car to Thao. Such is Kowalski's response to the man who tried to steal his car. Something very strange is afoot in the West today.

Thao is beaten up by an Asian gang, and Kowalski takes revenge by beating up one of the gang members. As we have seen, Whites are depicted as subservient to non-Whites, identify with them, and have impulses to work and fight for them. Kowalski starts to identify with the Asians, or with his captors. In psychology this is called the Stockholm syndrome. A well known example of this occurred with the kidnap victim Patty Hearst. She was kidnapped by a terrorist group, and she started to help and to agree with them. We see Kowalski undergo this same process during the film. Of course, this film represents in miniature the transformation in Whites' relation with non-Whites during the course of the twentieth century.

At one point in the film, a priest describes how it is sinful to kill during war, and later Kowalski admits that killing Asians during the Korean War has tortured his soul ever since. At the beginning of the film Kowalski rejects religion, but toward the end he has a conversion experience. In preparation for what will be in essence a suicide provocation of the gang, he goes to the priest and confesses some venial sins of his youth. Before going after the gang, he gives his silver metal earned fighting in the war to Thao. Kowalski goes to the house of the gang, provokes them, and they gun him down. The police discover that he was unarmed. The confrontation was self-sacrifice or compensation for his sins of killing during the war, and, likely, for his guilt feeling for a lifetime of racism or succumbing to the social body. This is evident in his giving the metal to Thao. Thao is the true hero, while Kowalski is just a miserable and condemned sinner, who can do no more than work, fight, and die for his master. In essence, the film shows the transformation of the traditional heroic battle against sin and the devil into the battle against in-group self-love, worthiness, or vanity; and by implication, a condemnation of out-group hostility, elitism or racism. Clint strikes a suicidal blow against feeling worthy, the condition he was in at the beginning of the film.

His death also exemplifies the sinner suffering for his sins, and even suffering at the hands of the sins themselves, though it probably would have been better if the Klan had killed him for being a "race" traitor. But his conversion to Christianity and moral conversion to multi-racialism complicates his status at the end of the film. He is clearly no longer a simple sinner being punished. There is an element of martyrdom in his death, and thus an element of the imitation of Christ or being a Christ-type, which is what martyrs are. That it was a suicide would elicit pity in most viewers, and this is a primary emotion in Christians' experience of Christ's passion or death. That he dies to redeem the sins of the social body is shown by one strong piece of symbolism. As Kowalski lies dying on the ground you see in his hand a military decoration he earned killing Koreans in the war. War is an example of out-group hostility or feeling worthy relative to the communists, so is thus a sin of the social body. His death/suicide, evoking pity, redeems himself or the social body of its original sins. After all, we can trace all racial tensions to earlier stages of history, right? At least according to modernist dogma.

That social body modesty is a driving force in modernism is shown by a quote from Susan Sontag: "During the last years Vietnam has been stationed inside my consciousness as a quintessential image of the suffering and heroism of the weak. But it was really America the strong that obsessed me-the contours of American power, of American cruelty, of American self-righteousness."[3] War is certainly no exercise in modesty. As can be seen in the opera *Lohengrin*, only the King and God get to be judge or righteous. Today Whites must defer to and be judged by non-Whites. Notice that it is common for non-Whites to judge Whites, while the reverse is seen as racism, as Kowalski suffers from at the beginning of the film. Kowalski's racism represents a sinful era of history, like the Old Testament, before the coming of the non-White redeemer who teaches Whites the virtue of social body modesty. The film is about the progress of an individual soul from sin to salvation through martyrdom or imitation of Christ. Of course, the viewer is supposed to see his own struggles for virtue and salvation mirrored in Kowalski's struggle and transformation. Whites have spent so many centuries being reprimanded by authority figures, that this is what feels good and natural in almost any form, even if it means suicide or death. Of course, this death was always viewed as the wages of sin.

Modern entertainment has not progressed beyond the medieval morality play. As should be clear, this is a very old impulse. In Spain during the sixteenth century, a woman went to the Inquisition and insisted that she was a sinner, and should be punished. They reviewed her sins and concluded that she was okay, and dismissed her. A few months later she came back and insisted that she was a terrible sinner and requested to be executed. They dismissed her again. She came back a third time and made the same claim and insisted that she be executed. Realizing that the situation was hopeless, the Inquisition acquiesced and burned her at the stake.

While *Gran Torino* took us up to heaven, the film that gets the award for hitting rock bottom is *Dances With Wolves* (1990). This film is certainly a great blow against feeling worthy.

Kevin Costner plays Lieutenant Dunbar, an officer in the army during the Civil War. He requests posting to the Army's

---

[3]William A. Rusher, "Will They Ever Learn?" Claremont, California: *The Claremont Review of Books*, Volume IV, Number 2, Spring 2004, 22.

westernmost fort. It turns out to be two mud brick buildings that are abandoned and falling apart. He is the only person there. That the military would assign an officer to an abandoned fort seems unlikely, but this is necessary for the rest of the plot. Left to his own devises he makes friends with the local Indians. Had he been with other soldiers he would have been forced to keep his distance.

An early scene shows that Dunbar is not a gung-ho 19th-century White man. Before Dunbar's journey, another officer asks him, "So, you're an Indian fighter?" Dunbar responds, "Excuse me?" An element of ambiguity is thus introduced into Dunbar's character. Except for Dunbar, the protagonist, all the other Whites are portrayed as stupid and crazy, but mostly vicious. For instance, the officer who assigns Dunbar to his post says, "I've peed in my pants," pulls out a gun, and shoots himself. This could almost be right out of Bosch.

When Dunbar arrives at the abandoned fort, he describes the surrounding countryside as being "Like no place on earth." Such hyperbole is common in the film to forward the modernist agenda. The film is propaganda from beginning to end, but that is the norm today. Even Nazi film makers would have blushed at some of the tactics used. After Dunbar meets his first Indian, he describes him as "magnificent." The first view that we have of an Indian camp is accompanied by majestic music. This is a real vision of grandeur and purity. Here is the goal of life, according to the film

Dunbar finds an injured White woman dressed in Indian clothing. He does not inquire how she got into this position and if she would rather go back to civilization, but merely takes her to the Indian camp and leaves her there. This is her true home and where Dunbar himself will eventually end up. Back at the Indian camp, the White woman says that she likes it there and is afraid that civilization will take her away.

Before we progress with the main plot involving Dunbar, we must stop and review two small scenes early in the film. One shows an unarmed man, who has stopped to eat lunch, killed by

Indians even though he has made no threatening gestures. The Indians shoot him full of arrows and scalp him. In the other scene, the Indians massacre a peaceful family of farmers who posed no threat. Those two introductory scenes are amazing in light of what happens later in the film. Most of the film shows the Indians as innocent victims of encroaching civilization. The essential brutality of the Indians, while portrayed, is never allowed to interfere with the propagandistic purpose of the film. It probably does not occur to most viewers that there is something wrong with these murders, so accustomed are they to masochistic social modesty from Hollywood. This is how much the West hates itself today. It just feels right, as similar perspectives of righteousness and modesty have for centuries.

After a few contacts with the Indians, Dunbar writes in his journal that the Indians are not, as he has heard, beggars, thieves, and "boogie men." Indeed, the film portrays them as sweethearts. Later, Dunbar becomes their friend and hunts with them. When they reach the bison herd, they find about a dozen dead in the field without their skins. They were killed by soulless White hunters. At least one Nazi film implied that Jews were soulless.

Dunbar starts to participate regularly in Indian life and even exchanges an article of clothing with an Indian. Dunbar says that it is a "good trade." Back at the fort, Dunbar dances around a fire Indian style and praises the Indians for their strong sense of community. As a narrator, Dunbar says that one day there will be "too many White people" in the area. The Indians rename Dunbar "Dances with Wolves" because they saw him playing or dancing with a wolf.

With his new name, Dunbar says that he has discovered who he really is. In religious conversion people commonly change their names. St Paul changed his name from Saul, and there are many examples of this in history. The film depicts this as an act of modesty for Dunbar. Through the White woman, Dunbar learns to speak the Indian language. As the result of this intimacy, he marries the White woman. This is a good example of reconciliation through sex, a tactic used in the animal kingdom.

By three quarters of the way through the film, he wears Indian clothing and is almost assimilated. This purported modesty increases as the film progresses.

During a visit to his camp, he discovers that it has been occupied by a fairly large military force. They think that he is an Indian, beat him and take him into custody. At first he agrees to speak English and tries to explain the situation, but the military personnel are hostile and accuse him of treason and "goin' injun." After a few minutes of this, he starts to speak in the Indian language and says that he will refuse to cooperate with the military. He is a rebel against sinful social vanity. They say that they will ship him back to another, larger installation and have him tried and hanged. As a military escort takes Dunbar back for trial, a group of his Indian friends attacks the unit. One of the Indians is wearing a US military hat. This shows us who is righteous and who ought to have sovereignty. It resembles Walt Kowalski giving his metal to Thao in *Gran Torino*. The entire military unit is killed. During their fighting the White soldiers have crazed looks on their faces and are portrayed as vicious while the Indians are portrayed as noble.

Dunbar is reunited with the Indians, his saviors. When Dunbar gets back to the Indian camp, he and his wife passionately kiss. They love one another in God or through the Indians, as is the truly righteous thing. Their love has been blessed by the Indians. The West now looks to the Indians as a model and for redemption, as the film has made clear. (A grade school teacher in California reported that the kids just love the Indians. They are the very picture of wild progress and redemption.) Dunbar says in a meeting with the Indians that it was good that the Indians killed the soldiers. In this film we see again militarism used in modernist or propagandistic purposes as in *Tears of the Sun*. Killing is fine as long as you kill the right people-representatives of Western civilization.

In one of the last scenes, Dunbar talks with an elderly Indian man. The Indian says that the old Dunbar no longer exists and that now he is an Indian. He has been reborn, as Dunbar implies two or three times in the film. As Christians wanted to imitate Jesus, now modernists want to imitate Indians. Dunbar describes the old Indian as an "extraordinary man." Again, hyperbole is used as propaganda and to forward modesty. Indians built teepees from animal skins and shot wooden arrows, while Western civilization built the Eiffel Tower and sent men to the moon, but this film presents the Indians as extraordinary. Even Nazi filmmakers would have had difficulty following this act.

Modern liberals are almost as intolerant as the Nazis; they just believe in demeaning a different group: Westerners who dispute the modernist agenda or the social body in general. To them, there seems to be something virtuous about suicide, the destruction of the drive toward sin or our sinful, immodest natures, as there was something virtuous about medieval flagellants.

The last scene in the film portrays the military pursuing Dunbar and the Indians into the snowy hills. The film implies that Dunbar and the Indians escaped. Text at the end of the film says that the Indians eventually came under White rule, and that "the American frontier was soon to pass into history." What is implied is that as long as the West was wild or irregular it was alive, or real and rebellious. But when it was settled or pressed down upon it was killed, and made a relic of history. It is no longer "The greatest place on earth."

Reversion to savagery and dancing around is righteous and understandable to modernists. It is an example of social modesty. If dancing with wolves is an ideal then the animal act of modern dance, and the rest of modernism, makes sense, in a dark and nonsensical sort of way. Traditionally, the progressive goal of popular culture was assimilation to God, now it is assimilation to non-Whites. This represents the vision of social modesty and virtue. It explains why *Dances With Wolves* is seen as progressive.

The plot of *Avatar* (2010) is almost identical to *Dances With Wolves*, with humanity representing Western civilization and blue aliens in the role of Indians. The human hero, Jake, joins the natives in the jungle to fight against the evil forces of humanity. Jake's former superior officer at one point says to Jake, "So what's it like being a traitor to your race?" This is a rehash of the modernist social humility or unworthiness that we saw in *Wolves*. The human race is unworthy to be fought for. As the ideal was to be a traitor to yourself, now it is to your species or the social body. There is a Bach's Cantata, "A Mighty Fortress is our God." If you want to get inside the fort, or in this case the jungle, then you need to be a traitor to your race, at least if you are White. Imagine that if there was a war between non-Blacks and Blacks, and a Black went over to the side of non-Blacks. Do you think Hollywood would make a movie romanticizing this? In other words, is it at all conceivable that God would fight on the side of the Devil? Not in this inhuman world. So the bad news is that we are not gods, but the good news is that this represents the victory of humanism. The Greeks observed that people were prone to self-deification, but this can and must be resisted.

As should be clear by now, what in part drives modernism are very strong patterns of emotion. Of these, the emotions of heroism and fidelity can be seen among apes. Seeing these among apes helps get them in focus among humans. It is common among apes for an individual to fight for or defend an individual with which he is familiar, or for which he has sympathy. This is such a powerful emotion among apes, that it has been found that an individual will defend a human he feels sympathy for against another unknown human. This is the case even if the known human starts the fight.[4] Notions of sympathy and fidelity trump the human idea of justice.

This entire scenario can be seen at work in modernism's theology of "race," in the next chapter. As Christians wanted to be faithful to God and had sympathy for Jesus, now non-Black Americans show deference towards Blacks. This emotion

---

[4]Frans De Waal, *Chimpanzee Politics*, 25th Anniversary Edition. (Baltimore: Johns Hopkins University, 2007).

trumps normal standards of justice. For instance, I once was speaking with a South African woman, and I said to her, "Since Apartheid came down, 30,000 Whites have been murdered by Blacks." She glared at me and simply said, "Their rights." Seeing that she defended Blacks at all costs, I dropped the subject. A study found that a White woman is ten times more likely to be killed by her spouse if married to a Black man than married to a White man. I sent this information to a White woman, and she thought that it was fine. Similarly, an organization published a study that found that half a million White Americans are attacked every year by Blacks (New Century Foundation). When the organization held a press conference to release this fact, only one newspaper reported the statistic. As with the South African woman, those in the media want to defend Blacks at all costs. Academics in criminology and elsewhere know about this, but do not talk about it publicly for fear of being accused of racism. The dogma today is to be faithful to Blacks no matter what, or no matter what human ideas of justice might be in other, larger, contexts. We have seen heroic impulses of Whites in other contexts, such as in the films *Tears of the Sun*, and *Avatar*. It got a big push by Hugo, who in *Les Miserables* portrays the lower classes as Christ-types and worthy of pity or sympathy. This was gradually expanded to include not just the poor but, as we have seen, pretty much all non-Whites.

The impulses of sympathy and the moral idea of being a traitor to yourself or to your own culture combine to create a toxic perspective. This helps to explain the apathy of many Americans in response to their country being invaded by high crime and hostile Mexicans. With little sense of civic survival left, the West's days are numbered unless it can break out of its masochistic prison.

Chapter 6

Modernism's Theology of "Race"

"Society made him do it!"

— Almost any attorney
U.S. society today displays a dominance hierarchy, with non-Blacks smiling at Blacks to appease and atone. Even a fraudulent accusation of "racism" can wreck a career, whether academic, business, or public sector. Courts have ruled it a crime or violation of federal regulation to "racially" offend someone, even when the offense is entirely in the eye of the accuser. Fear of such accusation makes non-blacks walk on eggshells when in the company of African Americans.

As society once passed judgment on African Americans and everyone else, now African Americans have the power to pass judgment on non-Blacks. Those African Americans who "play the race card" do so precisely because it works. Accusation alone suffices to convict. This is reminiscent of the following fragment of Greek poetry: "It is not granted unto men to fight the gods, or to pass judgment: no one has this right."[1] Similarly,

---

[1] M. L. West, trans., *Greek Lyric Poetry* (Oxford: Oxford University, 1993), 138.

135

in Pericles's Funeral Oration he said that "The blows of the enemy we must bear with courage: those of the gods, with resignation."[2] Most non-Blacks today are resigned to Black hostility. To deny an accusation of having caused "racial" offense brings terrible retribution. The following nineteenth century description of the status of criminals resembles how anyone accused of "racism" is seen today:

> He was a convict; that is, the creature who, on the
> social ladder, has no place, being below the lowest
> round. After the lowest of men, comes the convict.
> The convict is no longer, so to speak, the fellow of
> the living.[3]

Nowadays, anyone accused of "racism" is beyond the pale or outside of proper civil discourse, or in other words are so low as to be not human. In addition, it is taboo to pass judgment on the African-American community by mentioning its flaws, such as high crime rates, low test scores, or low net worth compared to income. They are seen as in this quotation from Les Miserables: "God has his instruments. He uses what tool He pleases. He is not responsible to man."[4]

This deference explains why modernists apparently hate Western culture. They falsely equate African-Americans with non-West or anti-West. Instead of the modernist hating himself, he hates the next best thing, Western civilization itself, because of the connection that exists in the mind. An example of such self-effacement can be found in a scene in the film version of the eighteenth century novel Dangerous Liaisons (1988), where a man and a woman are talking. The man says, "But I just don't feel worthy." The woman responds, "But it is when you don't feel worthy that you become worthy." Similarly, a

---

[2]H.D.F. Kitto, The Greeks (London: Penguin Books, 1957), 142.

[3]Ibid., 1216-17.

[4]Victor Hugo, Charles E. Wilbour, trans., Les Miserables (New York: Modern Library, 1992), 1216.

character in Les Miserable, after confessing his crimes says, "It is by degrading myself in your eyes that I elevate myself in my own."[5] Modernists today become worthy when they hate their own civilization, or feel unworthy in the face of non-Westerners. To consider oneself unworthy is the sure sign of social virtue today.

This impetus is the source of bowing and scraping from academics towards non-West. They find endless evidence of the superiority of non-Western cultures. Any academic who rejects anti-Western dogma and depicts the accomplishments of Western civilization risks being fired. Praising Western thought is rarely countenanced and usually dismissed with a skeptical sneer.

Such rejection of rational thought recalls how Christians once responded to the temptations of the body or to the confinements of sin. This, in turn explains African-American deification at the hands of modernists. It resembles the ancestor-deification of Hellenistic cities. As previously mentioned, the Vikings once worshiped trees as images of endurance. Similarly, modernists worship African Americans as images of endurance.

When Nelson Mandela was released from prison, a White South African said, "He's our God."[6] A journalist for *Newsweek* described U.S. President Obama as "sort of God."[7] A cover of *Newsweek* portrayed Obama as an Indian God and with the title "God of All Things."[8] In the film *Bruce Almighty* (2003) a Black male actor plays "God". In the film *Ghost* (1990), the ghost of a White person is resurrected in the body of a Black person in order to realize a relationship of love. Those who

[5]Victor Hugo, Charles E. Wilbour, trans., *Les Miserables* (New York: Modern Library, 1992), 1205.

[6]National Public Radio, 1990.

[7]John Bolton, "President Obama's Foreign Policy: An Assessment," *Imprimis*, October 2009, Volume 38, number 10, page 2. Reprinted by permission from *Imprimis*, a publication of Hillsdale College.

[8]*Newsweek*, Nov. 22, 2010.

suffer for the sins of society are thereby elevated to divinity.

Fidelity to the manifestations of God in African Americans, and loathing of Western civilization are the essential modernist virtues. This explains why so many recoil in horror at any mention of the government-sponsored racism of the Jim Crow era.

Modernists take on the responsibility of others' suffering. They are prone to feeling guilty about the Third World's higher aggression levels and African Americans' former status as slaves.

Modernism protests that almost everything suffers for the sins of Western civilization. Some believe that trees suffer for its sins. Others believe that whales suffer. Some are more ambitious and try to prove that the ozone layer suffers for their sins. They believe that it is impossible for non-Blacks to suffer for the sins of African Americans, because obviously African Americans suffer for the sins of the West and, like Jesus, African Americans are innocent. Modernists see African Americans as Jesus-like. "How they suffer!" There is no greater heresy than to claim that African Americans are collectively guilty of anything.

As it is painful for Christians to think of turning their backs on Jesus, so it is painful for modernists to think of turning their backs on African Americans, trees, whales, and so on. This would stop the progress to redemption. The vision of suffering is why modernism, when not raging against the sins of the West, is usually on the verge of tears. Modernism is driven by a vision of a number of angry Christ-types.

To them, Western culture is guilty. Modernism yearns for redemption and looks to the trees, whales, and African Americans for redemption and renewal through communion. If one person kills another, then a modernist will point to the killer, become misty, and say, "See how he suffers for our sins!" Then, "What can we do to help him?" This condoning perspective is different from the traditional one.

Modernists get their logic from the Bible. Therefore, conceptually, modernism and classicism are essentially identical;

they reach different conclusions only because they see cause and effect working in opposite directions. For example, modernism sees social policy creating homicidal tendencies, or human imperfection, as we saw in the fight in *Titanic*, while the traditional view sees homicidal tendencies creating social policy as can be seen in the nineteenth century.

In modernist imagination, the West suffers at the hands of its sins-as in Hieronymus Bosch's *The Garden of Earthly Delights*. In the famous medieval painting, a glutton is devoured by a huge stomach on legs. A sodomite is impaled by a Demon bird. A musician is tortured by his harp. Such reasoning sometimes appears in Classical myth. For instance, the Greek hero Neoptolemus commits homicide at an altar, and is himself later killed at an altar. And the mortal Semele falls in love with Zeus and demands that he show himself in all his glory. So he turns himself into a thunder bolt and this of course incinerates Semele. Similarly, Actaeon is out hunting with his dogs, and accidentally sees Artemis bathing. She becomes outraged and turns him into a stag, whereupon his dogs devour him.

These myths show how concerned the ancients were with morals. The use of this logic today, as we shall see, shows the depth it has penetrated in our culture. For instance, Western civilization erodes the ozone layer, so it suffers. Westerners cut down the trees, so they suffer. And African Americans attack non-Blacks because of the sins of the West. The West suffers at the hands of its sins. During the mid-twentieth century, the Hays film censorship code required that fictional sinners suffer for their fictional sins. The concept of sin followed by retribution is the source of modernist apocalyptic prophesies, like global warming. The film *The Day After Tomorrow* (2004) exemplifies the fear of sin. After years of unabated global warming, the greenhouse effect wreaks havoc around the globe in catastrophic hurricanes, tornadoes, tidal waves, floods, and, most ominously, the beginning of the next ice age. It is a warning of the fruits of social hubris or of feeling worthy.

The West's sinful social practice must consume them, so modernism rages against Western culture and criticizes society's temptations. Society's false desires cause the sufferings of Christ-types and take people off the righteous path of loving communion with trees, whales, and African Americans. In other words, such false desire or "false consciousness," breaks the bond or atonement between the West and its various suffering servants, redeemers, and saviors, as in Christian tradition the false desires of the body broke the bond with Jesus. To modernists, the trees have arrived to redeem humanity if humanity will just accept them. Those who turn their backs on the trees are evil. As Christians once were to love one another in God, to gain a higher strength, modernists love one another in the trees.

As impulses from the body were once seen as false and drove Christians down the wrong path, modernists see impulses from society as false because they drive people down the wrong path. The feeling of attachment that drives modernism is displaced desire for communion with a redeemer. Modernists desire redemption and look to the trees, whales, and African Americans for redemption and renewal through communion if they can just break society's grip.

Modernists think that African Americans suffer for Western civilization's sins, but that if non-Blacks accept Blacks and the West's guilt, then their sins will be forgiven and modernism will be righteous. Modernism's felt righteousness creates their hair-trigger sensitivity and placating yearning. They want to get right with the Lord and to attack anyone who gets in their way.

In the 1960s, trees and African Americans were added to the modernist pantheon and suddenly modernists found themselves surrounded by the unredeemed or heretics. As Westerners were once Christian warriors, modernists suddenly felt compelled to become warriors for the trees and African Americans and to work for their political elevation. Hence, they attack non-Blacks that are unredeemed or cut off.

Before 1960s, the body was the morally problematized object and seen as the location of agency. During the 1950s and

1960s, with the academic redemption of the body, notions of human agency or emotional motivation and evil were displaced to the public sphere, creating the modernist critique of social, governmental, and technological evils that are people's doom. As Christians had previously raged against the body, modernists now raged against society. As Christians were once vigilant against impulses from the body, modernists now are vigilant against impulses from the social body. As Christians were once in a constant state of protest against the body, modernists are now in a constant state of protest against society. The cry, "Babylon!" became "Society!" As the body had caused global warming, today the social body causes global warming. As the body was seen as the source of temptation and pollution, today the social body is seen as the source of pollution and temptation-the temptations of race and gender, for instance: "Don't you succumb to the urges of race and gender: that's the social body," says the modernist. The displacement of agency was a frequent concept in Homeric Greece. As Classical scholar E. R. Dodds noted in *The Greeks and the Irrational*, "unsystematized, nonrational impulses, and the acts resulting from them, tended to be excluded from the self and ascribed to an alien origin."[9] The belief in "society" is a form of animism and, as we have seen, results from the connection in the mind.

The concept of society as beyond human agency is a modernist invention that turns policy from a reflection of people's desires into an evil imposition that creates desires. Classicists, on the other hand, believe that the social body is a fiction, and that traditional policy-that is, policy before the 1960s-reflects public desires.

As Christians had purged or expelled the body, modernists expel the state. Modernists feel that society hems them in, and they want to be liberated. As Christians wanted to be rid of the body, modernists now want to be rid of the social body, society.

---

[9]E. R. Dodds, *The Greeks and the Irrational* (Berkeley: University of California, 1951), 17.

They believe in social reform instead of body reform. They displaced into the public sphere the metaphors they previously used to understand the body: "Don't succumb!" The urges of the social body are the source of all imperfection, suffering, and death.

In artistic representation, Jesus is usually portrayed either as triumphant, erect, and alert, or as suffering in bleeding agony. Modernism's view of African Americans vacillates between these two conceptualizations. When an African American is seen sleeping on the street, he is experienced as suffering for our social body's sins. When an African American is in college, he is seen as triumphant over non-Blacks' sins-a vision of Resurrection and Heaven. African Americans are burdened with the sins of all mankind, but they will be resurrected if modernists can just purge the social body and defeat it with love and communion.

Suffering occupies a prominent place in the Judeo-Christian imagination. The Jews suffered, the prophets suffered, Jesus suffered, the apostles suffered, and the martyrs suffered. Jesus warned Christians that they must be prepared to take up their cross and suffer. In addition, in Greek myth, Prometheus and Odysseus are long-suffering. Christ was the first archetypical victim in Western culture and today's victim archetypes are modeled on Him.

A recent TV advertisement about preventing violence said, "Violence has warning signs." It then showed a picture of a Hispanic boy with a tear running down his cheek. How he suffers! It is clear to certain Whites that they suffer at the hands of the sins themselves. In response, a common chant of modernism is, "They're going to change! Be Resurrected! If we can just crucify the social body!" As the Devil once conspired against Christians through the body, today the social body conspires against modernists and their various victims through the body. A bumper sticker during the 2004 national election read: BUSH/SATAN. Modernism never tires of alleging that Western culture is the primary medium of the social body, and thus is the source of all suffering and deviance in the world.

Christians once inspected, contemplated and mourned the rejection, wounds, and sufferings of Jesus, and hoped and worked for better days. Similarly, modernists today inspect, contemplate, and mourn the rejection, wounds and suffering of the trees and minorities, and hope and work for better days. Thus, many modernists feel drawn to social work instead of finishing schools, as did the elite in traditional Western culture.

Two recent books on feminism have titles that draw from Jesus imagery: *Reviving Ophelia* (1995) and *Ophelia Speaks* (1999). Jesus was first revived and then he spoke and pointed the way to redemption. Women were first released from the bondage of the social body, and now they speak pearls of wisdom, charms for redemption. The powerful emotions of modernism should make one suspicious. The obsessions of the 1950s turned into the obsessions of the 1960s.

A film title, *Malcolm X: Soldier of Righteousness*, reflects when Christians were soldiers of righteousness against the body. Similarly, there is a book entitled *Redemption Song: Mohammed Ali and the Spirit of the Sixties*. During the 1960s, modernists asked African Americans what kinds of sacrifices were necessary to make them happy, to atone for non-Black guilt, to redeem the West. As Jesus was reviled but proud, similarly gays and African Americans were reviled, but starting in the 1960s it was believed that they should be proud-gay pride and Black pride. *Ecce homo* means "behold the man," so starting during the 1960s, modernists pointed to African Americans and said, "behold the man." An image that loomed was that only a monster would partake in the flagellation and stigmatizing of Jesus, succumbing to the conspiring social body.

As Christians were once concerned about the progress of Jesus in their lives, today modernists are concerned about the progress of the African Americans in their lives. In this sense, modernism is progressive. If one proposes anything that gets in the way of that progress, modernists fly into a rage as they feel moral redemption or salvation slipping away.

Modernists need African Americans and the other victims for progress to occur. The universities have abandoned the study of the human condition (Classical studies, for instance), and are now devoted to the study of the various victims and their progress against society. Dinesh D'Sousa calls the movement of the 1960s the "Victim revolution."[10]

The universities have regressed to being medieval or religious institutions. During the Dark Ages, Roman roads were viewed as the product of the black arts. Similarly, today modernism views the biology of human variation as a black art because it stops progress. As noted earlier, one professor proposed making research into human variation a crime. As the body was once stigmatized or banned, today the social body, which stops progress, should be banned. As Christians were once angry with the body, today modernists are angry with the social body. Before the 1950s the religious cowered and said "God is angry at us." Starting during the 1960s modernists cowered and said, "African Americans are angry at us," and thus desired atonement.

The more violent African Americans become, the more this excites modernism, because it is divine retribution. One can imagine Jesus casting sinners into hell. A book titled *Green Rage* justifies terrorism by environmentalists (as if Christian warriors). Modernism supports violence as punishment for sin.

Because of the violence and debauchery of modernism, it contains what Classical scholars would call a Dionysian element. Several scholars have noted the similarity between ancient Greek religion and contemporary modernist religious culture. As Classical scholar Martin P. Nilsson noted:

> There [is] seen...a seventh figure clad in a Dionysiac costume-boots and fawnskin. He is Iacchos. Iacchos is a personification of the Iacchic

[10]Dinesh D'Sousa, *Illiberal Education: The Politics of Race and Sex on Campus* (New York: Vintage Books, 1992), 1.

cry heard in the great procession, which went
from Athens to Eleusis in order to celebrate the
Mysteries. The gay revels, the merry cries, and
the light of the torches in this procession were
reminiscent of the festivals of Dionysus, and the
name of Iacchos suggested the second name of this
god, Bacchos. So Iacchos was represented in the
likeness of Dionysus.[11]

Thus, modernists portray African Americans in the likeness of Dionysus, as irresponsible hedonists, a view shared by
much of the public. I once saw a book entitled, *Why Black
Folks Like to Yell*. In the San Francisco area, I have twice seen
African Americans yelling with hostility at each other on the
street, and non-Black bystanders simply smiling. As Classical
scholar David Sacks noted, the Greek gods are concentrations
of energy.[12] Similarly, modernists see African Americans as
mindless concentrations of energy, as well as victim archetypes.
Modernists have heaped the West's sins upon African Americans, who creak under the weight. The religious motivation for
the indulgent emotions of modernism is reminiscent of the religious festivals of ancient Egypt. As David O'Connor noted
regarding the festival for the arrival of a god:

Such festivals were occasions for public participation and rejoicing, and they established an
important link between the deity and its community. Food and drink were distributed to the
populace, and ordinary rules of decorum were
often ignored. As one scholar has described it, the
behavior of the participants was "excessive and
unrestrained, be it eating, drinking, sex, or all three

---

[11] Martin P. Nilsson, *Greek Folk Religion* (Philadelphia: University of Pennsylvania, 1972), 47.

[12] David Sacks, *A Dictionary of the Ancient Greek World* (Oxford: Oxford
University, 1995).

at once." These activities were probably associated
with that "induced, ecstatic state" thought to
facilitate communion between humans and the
gods, or between the living and the dead.[13]

With the redefinition of African Americans as redeemers,
modernists started, as part of their attempts at communion and
imitation of ghetto culture, to eat, drink, take drugs, and have
unmarried sex.

Modernists look on and yearn for redemption, especially
when so much fun or revels are to be had. For modernism, the
joy of redemption correlates with the fun of the body. Thus,
modernists look for redemption to the trees, African Americans, whales, and so on, with smiling joy, and seek connection
or communion with God, the "all-powerful" and the "all-fun"
concentration of energy.

Modernism also spawns exaggerated environmentalism. As
Christians once dreamed about Jesus and the angelic perfect
body, today they dream about the redeeming perfect bodies of
nature. Modernists feel revived by nature. As Christians are refreshed by the connection with Jesus, modernists are refreshed
by connections with trees and African Americans, whom they
see as somehow more primitive or earthy. Thus, they often start
to beam when they are in African Americans' company. In making a connection with African Americans, they feel progress.

As Jesus was "the heart's desire," similarly trees and African
Americans are the heart's desire. As Christians used to be lost
in Jesus, now modernists are lost in African Americans. One
White girl said to me that African Americans are her favorite
people. It was odd that Asians were not her favorite. In the
Bible, a fallen woman cleaned Jesus' feet with her tears, and so
He forgave her sins. I once saw a White televangelist kneel and
use his tie to clean the shoe of an African American preacher so
that the televangelist's sins would be forgiven.

---

[13]David O'Connor, "Architecture of Infinity-The Egyptian Temple." *Ar-
chaeology Odyssey*, September, 1999, 46-47.

As Christians were once dead to the world and alive in Christ, modernists are now dead to society and alive in African Americans, trees, and whales, and seek their moral resurrection through these agents. As Jesus had more than one vote in the lives of Christians, an African-American lawyer suggested that African Americans should have more than one vote during elections.

One professor described multiculturalism as "summoning," just as Jesus was summoning. Modernists are summoned to make progress. Christians say that Christianity is not a religion, but a relationship. Similarly, modernists say that their ideology is not a belief system but a series of relationships that summon them to the goal of progress, redemption and atonement. If a non-Black has not accepted African Americans as special, he is viewed as evil. He rejects the summons and turns his back, and so is cut off. As Christians once looked to Jesus for guidance, modernists now look to African Americans. As Jesus was in charge and made the summons, today African Americans are in charge, and the modernists listen to the summons for progress.

In ancient Athens, to help achieve political acceptance or power, the tyrant Pisistratus dressed a tall woman as Athena, put her on a cart, and marched behind her up the Acropolis, demonstrating extreme or literal atonement. During the 1960s, modernists dressed African Americans as Jesus, and marched behind them down the street. Cleopatra crafted the image of Mark Antony as the god Bacchus in order to achieve certain political ends. Similarly, today modernists have crafted the image of African Americans as suffering servants in order to achieve certain political ends-their own political empowerment.

There is no question that the African-American community suffered collectively during the Jim Crow era. So it was easy to attach this suffering to the sins of the West to be able to formulate a modernist political strategy. This reveals the heart of contemporary political discourse in the United States. Religion is the heart of culture and politics. As the heart pumps blood to the extremities of the body, religious belief pumps power to people and groups of people.

During the 1960s, modernism ascended to the moral high ground by crying out, "They suffer for our sins!" Listeners thought: That sounds compelling. They must be right. African-American blood is shed for our guilt. African Americans are the suffering servants. Non-Blacks are evil, and African Americans are innocent or good. Non-Blacks must commune with or accept African Americans to be redeemed, for progress to occur. It is the social body that takes us off the righteous path.

Such reasoning has been sinking in deeper ever since and is visible on every college campus. Many academic departments today criticize the social body and try to figure out how to repress, subvert, and transcend it: "Subvert the Dominant Paradigm!"

Christians are awed by Jesus' suffering and resurrection and all that these mean to them. Modernists often feel reverence and attachment when in the company of African Americans because of how African Americans function in the narrative of modernism's moral and physical regeneration. The moral standing of non-Blacks depends on the condition of African Americans. The resurrection or enculturation of the latter, the defeat of the social body, will facilitate the resurrection, both moral and physical, of the former.

Although few modernists are eager to associate with African Americans on a basis of friendly equality, they want to work for the image of suffering in their mind's eye, so they go into social work. In their minds, when the social body has been defeated, and African Americans become acculturated and are no longer hostile, the Apocalypse will subside, and Heaven will triumph.

With the displacement of evil and human agency to the public sphere, not only trees and African Americans are Christ-types, but many others strive for rhetorical victimization as well. Modernists are eloquent in their suffering or victimization by the social body-by their parents, for instance, the source of imperfection.

Modernists have displaced the Jesus victim narrative onto themselves and onto objects in their environment. The individuals or groups that have the best victim credentials attract the most attention and sympathy. This results in competition between people and groups to see who can produce the best proof of victimization and so be qualified to receive the largest sacrifices: "We're righteous so we're entitled!" they chant. This is the reasoning behind government entitlements. As Jesus was entitled, so are we.

Because modernists suffer, they think that they are justified in being demanding and abusive, expressive of their aggression. As Jesus was justified in being outraged against the body or sin, so modernists are outraged against the social body that causes suffering and imperfection. Modernism whispers to itself, "I suffer and feel angry because of the social body, because of employers, technology, belligerent acquaintances, nuclear energy, and so on." During the 1970s, a businessman said, "People need stop crying and to start sweating." As technology is a modernist specter of evil, similarly an unfriendly neighbor is evil and worthy of attack. Criminals justify their actions with narratives of suffering.

This theme, lack of personal responsibility plus innocent victimization by external forces, is a common way of framing experience of the world. Dr. Thomas Sattler, a dermatologist, says that it is common for people to attribute skin problems to stress. The social body causes our wounds and justifies our anger. An African American speaker said that African Americans are irresponsible parents because of genetic engineering by Whites. Modernists blame society and so justify aggression. The example is typical of the causality of popular thought. Recall the socialization of sin. Today, it is easy to justify aggression. All one has to do is play the victim card, no matter how trivial. A woman spilled hot coffee on herself at a McDonald's restaurant, sued, and won.

This new moral schema of being victimized promotes fertility, or anti-social rebellion, in people's interpersonal relations, the medium for the intrusive social body. Once in a restaurant, another diner said to me, "If you find a hair in your food, sue their pants off!" We see this justification for deviance in ancient Greece. The Greeks believed that the god Hermes would steal cattle at night. So when this happened, farmers would say, "Ah, Hermes." Similarly, today when a crime happens, modernists say, "Ah, society." This is an example of the animism noted earlier.

One sign of the new metaphysics of fertility and social body rebellion is that today modernists say that every child is above average and demands to feel good or empowered instead of adhering to a standard, and feeling accomplished in that way. According to modernist dogma, traditional social standards are the social body, create imperfection and suffering, and should be repressed. Modernists often attribute academic weakness to an inability to take tests. It is clearly the social body's fault, just as it causes our skin problems. Today, modernism allows no one to say anything that does not make people feel good or fertile. If you propose that someone needs to live up to standards, the person will often react with anger. This is the source of modernist leveling. Modernism says that because we suffer, our desire to attack those who cause our suffering is morally justified. Modernists justify every negative urge with the narrative of suffering, instead of that narrative compelling them to adapt themselves to standards, as was traditional.

John Stott describes how Christianity inspires such a sense of heroic urgency within modernism. He writes:

> Christianity is a rescue religion. It declares that God has taken the initiative in Jesus Christ to deliver us from our sins.... There is no conquest without the Cross.[14]

---

[14]John R. W. Stott, *Basic Christianity* (London: Inter-Varsity, 1971), 81, 86.

Modernists confirm that they are trying to rescue people from their sins of succumbing to the hubris of society and urge them to accept any one of the modernist redeemers. With this acceptance and empowerment through dependent rank comes heroic status, enabling one to conquer anything. We see this idea in ancient Athens. As Classical scholar Martin P. Nilsson noted:

> [A god] came to Athens in 420 B.C., being intro-
> duced by Telemachos of Acharnae and received by
> the poet Sophocles, who because of this was made
> a hero under the name of Dexion, the Receiver.[15]

Similarly, modernists have much heroic energy because they have received the gods, are in a state of communion; in Christian context they are redeemed and righteous. As one Christian observed, "When you are saved, you are King!" So modernists point to classicists and exclaim, "You're still in your sins!" and "We're Kings because we're righteous!" or empowered.

Once a modernist has received his savior, he does not want to let go. We see this sense of attachment in newly Christianized ninth-century Germany. The Heliand was the telling of the Gospel for that German population. The author felt compelled to make concessions to the pagan religion of his audience. In the scene when Roman soldiers come to arrest Jesus, the Heliand portrays fierce swordplay to defend Jesus.[16] (Swordplay is not in the original.) In a spirit similar to Germanic heroism, in the United States today fierce resistance arises when a lumber company tries to harvest trees. Radical environmentalists put metal spikes in trees to ruin chainsaws and injure loggers.

There is another similarity between medieval religion and modernism. In the Middle Ages, Germanic peoples retained a

---

[15]Martin P. Nilsson, *Greek Folk Religion* (Philadelphia: University of Pennsylvania, 1972), 94.

[16]G. Ronald Murphy, *The Saxon Savior* (New York. Oxford University, 1989)

pagan belief that dangerous elves would harm people and live-
stock, so the church developed a set of Christianized charms
or chants to combat them. Similarly, non-Black males, who
are seen as today's social body, are viewed as harming things.
They harm whales, trees, ozone layer, and, of course, African
Americans. As the Catholic Church developed chants against
the elves, modernism has developed chants against non-Black
males, to ward off the social body, the source of threatening
evil.

In antiquity, people often compared gods to make a point
and to clarify their natures. For instance, Plutarch said that
Dionysus resembled the Egyptian god Osiris. Similarly, in the
1960s and '70s, when feminists tried to make their points, it was
common for them to say that women were "like Blacks." Feminists made this comparison in order to help clarify women's
nature as fellow suffering servants-as "The Goddess," as described on a bumper sticker. They, too, were to be part of the
same Pantheon, to be received as redeemers, revered, liberated,
and viewed as beautiful. More recently, homosexuals who view
their gender preference as ethno-political self-identity compare
themselves to African Americans in seeking the same deference, privilege, and coercive power. Homer also uses displaced
mythological narrative to create vivid characters. As Classical
scholar Seth L. Schein (1984) noted about the *Iliad*:

> The freedom with which Homer transfers to Pa-
> troklos and Hektor mythological motifs and dra-
> matic roles traditionally associated with Achilles
> and Memnon has suggested to some scholars that
> these two characters are creations of Homer.[17]

Similarly, the creation of the oral and written myths of the
suffering of African Americans, women, and homosexuals is
the result of the free-associative imagination of modernism.

---

[17]Seth L Schein, *The Mortal Hero: An introduction to Homer's Iliad*
(Berkeley: University of California, 1984), 27.

Anything that can be assimilated to a Christ-type usually is. We see this with the holocaust. Evidence that modernists experience the holocaust as a Christ-type is the strong reaction today from some western governments to individuals who deny that it happened. A movement called Historical Revisionism tries to disprove the holocaust. The historicity of the holocaust is undeniable, but it should be subject to normal critical review, without its critics being persecuted and imprisoned, as they are in Germany. As denying Jesus could get you killed in the early modern era, denying the holocaust today can result in prison time from some governments. Incidentally, these perspectives on the Holocaust are not mutually exclusive. The Holocaust can still be a Christ-type even though it actually happened.

This ambivalence helps explain the vacillation of modernism on the issue of the Jews and Israel. In the context of the holocaust, Jews are victims, and everyone wants to defer to and rescue them. In the context of the conflict between Israel and Palestine, Jews are oppressors, and modernism is critical of Jews defending themselves. Because modernists experience everything as either a Christ-type or the anti-Christ, they cannot formulate consistent foreign policy. There is a conflict between the historical victimization of the Jews and their modern image as oppressors, and modernism cannot work its way out of the dilemma. All a group need do is show their wounds, as do the Palestinians, and modernists accept their victim status. This tends to usurp historical claims, as from the Jews. Because the standards to achieve victim status are fairly low, modernism spends time running back and forth.

In *Les Miserables*, there is a scene where a young couple is in love and sitting on a bench. The woman leans over and the outline of her bosom becomes clear. The man turns his gaze away to avoid exposure to the body. We see the same thing today in modernism's relation with African Americans. If a modernist hears an unpleasant fact like, for instance, one in three African American men will eventually spend time in prison, he or she will not face it, and will turn the gaze away from this temptation from the social body. Negative thoughts about African Americans come from the social body, so are to be banished from our minds.

Modernists so want to see African Americans as great that they have created a show for themselves. Most of the African-American middle and upper class is a product of government hiring, the military and racial quotas. This impulse can be seen in history. The ancient Sumerians would dress up one of their gods, take him on boat rides and feed him lavish meals. In ancient Athens, the people made a 40-foot statue of Athena made of gold and ivory. The natural human impulse is to dress up and make a spectacle of where ever perceived power is. Through dependent rank, there is indirect self-empowerment.

As the heart pumps blood to the body, religion, pumps power to people. God and religion are fundamentally about universal power, so human or earthly power is seen as a subset of this. Tinkering with religion always results in changes with human values and politics.

Chapter 7

Conclusion

It should be the highest ambition of every American to extend
his views beyond himself, and to bear in mind that his conduct
will not only affect himself, his country, and his immediate pos-
terity; but that its influence may be co-extensive with the world,
and stamp political happiness or misery on ages yet un-born.

— George Washington

I know of no safe depository of the ultimate powers of the society but the people themselves. And if we think them not enlightened enough to exercise their control with a wholesome discretion, the remedy is not to take it from them, but to inform their
discretion by education. This is the true corrective of abuses of
constitutional power.

— Thomas Jefferson

Recall from the introduction the professor who said that the
Greeks understood things with a clarity that we have lost. Now
we see why. modernism, as we have seen in the films, is so lost
in fantasy that we are stumbling around and do not know which
way is up or down. While a few professors in evolutionary psychology and primatology have made progress in understanding
the human condition, their insights are published only in text-

books and journals. Their ideas are too politically incorrect to find common currency, especially among liberal arts professors. One professor said that Harold Bloom's book *The Closing of the American Mind*, while a good seller, had no impact on liberal arts departments. As it took a full two centuries to overthrow the virtue ethic, it will probably take a similar effort, though not necessarily that much time, to overthrow the far more comfortable and mythic dogmas of modernism. Communication is faster today than earlier, and literacy rates are higher.

In chapter one I was able to describe and defend humanism in art in about 20 pages, while to describe the fantasy of modernism took about 8 times as many pages. The right answer is always simple and clear while the wrong answer can go on forever. For example, there is only one right answer to the problem 2+2. The number of wrong answers is infinite.

Werner Jaeger was a Classics professor at Harvard during the early to mid twentieth century. In his *Paideia: the Ideals of Greek Culture* he makes the ethnocentric claim that only the West has culture. In other words, it was the Greeks who discovered the balance between form and content described in chapter one. While other groups stumbled from one fantasy to another, as we see in the fictional tribe in *Avatar*, and simply tried to massacre their neighbors, the Greeks were the first to discipline the mind and body and to coordinate them. To be specific, the Greeks discovered what we today call high culture. High culture, as we have seen, results from a rationalization of nature, as in the paintings of Claude, and the body, as in the art of Michelangelo. This objectivity also resulted in science. Nonwestern people either live more in the body, like most tribes, or in the mind, like the Eastern religions. The Greeks and their cultural descendants, Western civilization, were the first to strike the right balance. We live our lives surrounded by the benefits of this in science and technology.

Culturally however, things are different today. Most have all but abandoned high culture as an ideal. By inverting Platonism, placing nature over virtue, we have regressed to savagery, as also can be seen in *Dances with Wolves* and *Avatar*. Today's moral structure, as seen in film, is self-destructive or irrational. It reminds you of the Potlatch ceremony practiced by indigenous peoples of the Pacific Northwest Coast. It was originally a gift-giving tradition. But it turned into the custom of burning their belongings in order to show their wealth and generosity. This sounds strangely familiar. We still have minds and bodies, but they are largely dislocated from a goal of enlightened unity. Depending upon context, either our bodies jerk our minds around, or our minds jerk our bodies around.

We need to reestablish the right balance, but of course with the mind discovering and forming the rules. If we follow only our instincts, as many do today, we descend to barbarism. As Victor Hugo was quoted in chapter one, "Proportion his song to his nature, and you shall see!" The mind must do the forming, but not everyone has equal mental faculties, as Beethoven was quoted in this book's front matter.

The American founding fathers knew this. They had a traditional Platonist philosophy, which placed the mind in control of the will and appetites. When this ideal reigned, in the eighteenth and early nineteenth centuries, the West had a beautiful and great culture. But after the '48 revolution in Europe, the masses became more assertive and the balance was destroyed. As Brahms said when he heard Mahler's first symphony: "Is this the future of music?" Reed, a Schubert biographer, said that early Romantic music is better than late Romantic music, and I would agree, with the exception of Wagner. We see a similar disintegration in the other arts with the rise of naturalism in fiction and painting. In this period, suffrage was granted to unintelligent, uneducated, and poor men. This helped destroy the balance and the entirety of Western culture built on that balance.

We need to have the mind in control, and to have the kind of value system or hierarchy as earlier. The bad news is that society needs a mechanism to suppress the worst in human nature. The good news is that doing so will re-establish real justice and thus peace and harmony. During the eighteenth century, class hierarchy or elitism suppressed the worst of human nature, but today class hierarchy is dead and cannot be revived. Still, we must somehow return to rejecting our animal aspect, and individuals dominated by brute instinct, as funny or dismissed.

One possible approach would be to require people to take classes in the history of political philosophy, and then pass a test in political knowledge in order to vote. If a person cannot write a 10-page paper describing political positions, then he has no right having an influence in politics. As one professor said, "Confused writing is confused thought." We do not want confused people electing our representatives as we do today. Such ignorant demagoguery from the media contributes to the election of charismatic but inept political leaders.

We could even pass a law requiring people who cannot vote to salute those who can. If this seems peculiar, notice that nowadays U.S. society and government demand that non-Blacks defer to Blacks, and we have seen how destructive that is of morals. It would be a positive change to have the ignorant recognized as such and made to defer to their more educated superiors, instead of imagined ones. Something like this would help get the lower class, and for that matter most peoples' egos, back under control, and distribute power to where natural justice demands. We have seen the fruits of the inversion of Platonism. It is time to return to respecting virtue.

If we put the mind back in charge of our culture and politics, we will see the victory of humanism once again. We will have achieved Thomas Jefferson's ideal of a "natural aristocracy" or the right balance between the mind and body.[1]

---

[1] For further reading, see Richard Smith and Richard London, *Religion of Macho* (Bloomington IN: Author House, 2008). Also recommended is Jennifer Homans, *Apollo's Angels* (New York: Random House, 2010).

Bibliography

Allen, Robert C. "The Movies in Vaudeville: Historical Context of the Movies as Popular Entertainment." *The American Film Industry.* Tino Balio, Ed. Madison: University of Wisconsin Press, 1985.

Bauerlein, Mark. *The Dumbest Generation: How the Digital Age Stupefies Young Americans and Jeopardizes our Future.* New York: Penguin, 2008.

Blackburn, Simon. *Oxford Dictionary of Philosophy.* New York: Oxford University Press, 2008.

Bordes, Philippe. *Jacques-Louis David: Empire to Exile.* New Haven: Yale University Press, 2005.

Bretell, Richard. *Museum Masterpieces: The Metropolitan Museum of Art.* DVD lecture series. Chantilly, VA: The Teaching Company, 2007.

Bolton, John. "President Obama's Foreign Policy: An Assessment". *Imprimis*, October 2009, p. 2. Volume 38, number 10. Reprinted by permission from Imprimis, a publication of Hillsdale College.

Bruce, Vicki, and Andy Young. *In the Eye of the Beholder.* Oxford, England: Oxford University Press, 1998.

Chilvers, Ian. *The Oxford Dictionary of Art.* New York: Oxford University Press, 2004.

Cohen, Selma Jeanne, Ed. *Dance as a Theater Art.* Hightstown, NJ: Princeton Book Company, 1992.

Crystal, David. *The Cambridge Biographical Encyclopedia.* New York: Cambridge University Press, 1998.

Daly, Martin, and Margo Wilson. *Homicide.* New York: Aldine De Gruyter, 1988.

De Vecchi, Pierluigi. "Difficulty/ease and studied casualness in the work of Raphael." *Raphael: Grace and Beauty.* Milano: Skira Editori, 2001.

De Waal, Frans. *Chimpanzee Politics*, 25th Anniversary Edition. Baltimore: The Johns Hopkins University Press, 2007.

Durgnat, Raymond & John Kobal. *Greta Garbo.* New York: E. P. Dutton and Co., 1967.

Etcoff, Nancy. *Survival of the Prettiest.* New York: Double Day, 1999.

Fears, J. Rufus. *Books That Have Made History.* Audio-tape lecture series. Chantilly, VA: The Teaching Company, 2005.

Getty, J. Paul. *As I See It: The Autobiography of J. Paul Getty.* Los Angeles: Getty Publications, 2003.

Gill, Meredith J. *Augustine in the Italian Renaissance: Art and Philosophy from Petrarch to Michelangelo.* New York: Cambridge University Press, 2005.

Glad, John. "Eugenics and the Public". *The Mankind Quarterly.* Fall-Winter 2009, Volume L, no. 1 & 2, p. 120.

Greenberg, Robert. *How to Listen to and Understand Great Music*, 3rd Edition. DVD lecture series. Chantilly, VA: The Teaching Company, 2006.

Guelzo, Allen. "Hero, Standing." *Imprimis*, May/June, 2009. Volume 38, Number 5/6, page 4. Reprinted by permission from Imprimis, a publication of Hillsdale College.

Guest, Ivor. *The Paris Opera Ballet*. Alton, England: Dance Books, 2006.

Hashiloni-Dolev, Yael. *A Life (Un) Worthy of Living: Reproductive Genetics in Israel and Germany*. Dordrecht, The Netherlands: Springer, 2010.

Henslin, James. *Social Problems*. Englewood Cliffs, N.J: Prentice-Hall, 1990.

Homans, Jennifer. *Apollo's Angels: A History of Ballet*. New York: Random House, 2010.

Hyde, Melissa & Mark Ledbury. *Rethinking Boucher*. Los Angeles: Getty Publications, 2006.

Hugo, Victor. Charles E. Wilbour, Trans. *Les Miserables*. New York: Modern Library, 1992.

Idaho Statesmen, February 15, 2010, p. C1.

James, Henry. *The American*. New York: Signet Classics, 1965.

Janson, H.W. *History of Art*. Englewood Cliffs, N.J: Prentice-Hall, 1969.

Jewell, Richard. *The Golden Age of Cinema: Hollywood 1929-1945*. Malden, Mass.: Blackwell Publishing, 2007.

Jones, H. Stuart. *Ancient Writers on Greek Sculpture*. Chicago: Argonaut, Inc., Publishers, 1966.

Jover, Manuel. *Ingres*. Paris: Editions Terrail/Edigroup, 2005.

Kohler, Joachim. Steward Spencer, Trans. *Richard Wagner: The Last of the Titans*. New Haven: Yale University Press, 2004.

Lovejoy, Arthur O. *The Great Chain of Being*. Cambridge, Mass.: Harvard University Press, 1964.

McKenzie, Kevin. "Bringing Magic to Center Stage: The Art of American Ballet Theater." Nancy Ellison. *In Classic Style: The Splendor of American Ballet Theater*. New York: Rizzoli International Publications, Inc., 2008.

McKitrick, Eric L., Ed. *Slavery Defended: The Views of the Old South*. Englewood Cliffs, N.J.: Prentice Hall, 1963.

Michel, Regis. *Le beau ideal ou l'art du concept*. Paris, 1989.

Muller, Ulrick & Peter Wapnewski. *Wagner Handbook*. Cambridge, Mass.: Harvard University Press, 1992.

Murray, Charles. *Real Education*. New York: Crown Forum, 2008.

National Public Radio, "All Thing Considered," June 18, 1990.

New Century Foundation. *The Color of Crime*. Download available at: www.amren.com.

Nichols, Ashton. *Emerson, Thoreau, and the Transcendentalist Movement*. Audio-Tape lecture series. Chantilly, VA: The Teaching Company, 2006.

Nichols, Roger. "Lord of misrule: Chopin the rebel". Liner notes for CD entitled, *Chopin*, pianist Simon Trpceski. European Union: EMI Records, 2007.

Nitti, Patrizia; Marc Restellini; and Claudio Strinati, Ed. *Raphael: Grace and Beauty*. Milano: Skira Editori, 2001.

Ostwald, Peter F. "Johanness Brahms, Solitary Altruist." Walter Frisch, Ed. *Brahms and His World*. Princeton: Princeton University Press, 1990.

Pestritto, Ronald J. *Woodrow Wilson and the Roots of Modern Liberalism.* Lanham MD: Rowman & Littlefield Publishers, Inc, 2005.

Pliny the Elder. K. Jex-Blake, Trans. *The Elder Pliny's Chapters On The History Of Art.* Kessinger Publishing. Reprint of, New York: The Macmillan Co, 1896.

Pollard, A. Edward. "Black Diamonds." Eric L. Mckitrick, Ed. *Slavery Defended: the views of the Old South.* Englewood Cliffs, NJ: Prentice-Hall, 1963.

Price, S.R.F. *Rituals and Power: The Roman Imperial Cult in Asia Minor.* Cambridge: Cambridge University Press, 1984.

Reed, John. *Schubert: The Final Years.* London: Faber and Faber, 1972.

Reynolds, Sir Joshua. *Discourses.* New York: Penguin, 1992.

Roslavleva, Natalia. *Era of the Russian Ballet.* London: Victor Gollancz LTD, 1966.

Ross, Janice. *San Francisco Ballet at Seventy-Five.* San Francisco: Chronicle Books LLC, 2007.

Sachs, Harvey. *The Ninth: Beethoven and the World in 1824.* New York: Random House, 2010.

Sapolsky, Robert. Professor of Neurology, Stanford University. *Biology and Human Behavior: The Neurological Origins of Individuality.* Audio-Tape Lecture Series. Chantilly, VA: The Teaching Company, 1996.

Schorske, Carl E. *Fin-De-Siecle Vienna: Politics and Culture.* New York: Vintage Books, 1981.

Siepman, Jeremy. *Chopin: The Reluctant Romantic.* Boston: Northeastern University Press, 1995.

Spotts, Fredrick. *Bayreuth: A History of the Wagner Festival*. New Haven: Yale University Press, 1994.

Stoddard, Lothrop. *The Revolt Against Civilization*. New York: Charles Scribner's Sons, 1923.

Thomson, David. *The New Biographical Dictionary of Film*. New York: Alfred A. Knopf, 2002. And the Fifth Edition, 2010.

Tolstoy, Leo. Richard Pevear & Larissa Volokhonsky, trans. *Anna Karenina*. New York: Penguin, 2000.

Toman, Rolf. *Baroque: Architecture, Sculpture, Painting*. h.f. ullmann, 2007.

Valiunas, Algis. "Shall We Fight for Kind and Country?" *Claremont Review of Books*, Volume X, Number 1, Winter 2009/10.

Vasari, Giorgio. Julia Bondanella and Peter Bondanella, Trans. *Lives of the Artists*. New York: Oxford University Press, 2008.

Vieira, Mark A. *Irving Thalberg: Boy Wonder to Producer Prince*. Berkeley, CA: University of California Press, 2010.

Vyse, Stuart A. *Believing in Magic: The Psychology of Superstition*. New York: Oxford University Press, 1997.

Weaver, Robert L. "The Consolidation of the Main Elements of the Orchestra: 1470-1768." *The Orchestra*, Joan Peyser, Ed. Milwaukee, WI: Hal Leonard Corp, 2006.

Winckelmann, Johann Joachim. Harry Francis Mallgrave, Trans. *History of the Art of Antiquity*. Los Angeles: Getty Publications, 2006.

Wittkower, Rudolf. *Art and Architecture in Italy 1600-1750: II. High Baroque*. New Haven, CN: Yale University Press, 1999.

Backintyme

30 Medford Drive
Palm Coast FL 32137-2504
860-468-9631

See our complete list of books at:
http://backintyme.com/publishing.php

Order extra copies of this book at:
http://backintyme.com/ad412.php

www.ingramcontent.com/pod-product-compliance
Lightning Source LLC
LaVergne TN
LVHW092316080426
835509LV00034B/471